The Artist's Table

ACKNOWLEDGEMENTS

Utmost gratitude is owed to the master chefs who have contributed
their expertise and creativity to this project. Others also generously
contributed in many ways, among them Meesha Halm and
Maura Carey Damacion, Lisa Khoury, Keith Webb and Ysabel Lightner,
Hugo Rizzoli and the recipe testers, Gay, Phyllis, Rita, Linda, Don,
Rick, Anette, Margaret, Summer, Elisabeth, and Amanda. For sage, inventive
advice throughout the project, I am grateful to Frances P. Smyth.

First published in USA 1995 by Collins Publishers San Francisco
Copyright © 1995 National Gallery of Art
Editor: Meesha Halm
Design: Kari Perin
Design and Production Coordination: Kristen Wurz
Calligraphy: Jane Dill
Library of Congress Cataloging-in-Publication Data
The artist's table : a cookbook by master chefs
inspired by paintings in the National Gallery of Art /
edited and compiled by Carol Eron.
p.   cm.
Includes bibliographical references and index.
ISBN 0-00-225071-3
1. Cookery.   2. Dinners and dining--Illustrations.   3. Painting.
4. National Gallery of Art (U.S.)   I. Eron, Carol.
TX714.A78   1995
641.5--dc20   CIP 95-16676

Printed in Italy
1 3 5 7 9 10 8 6 4 2

The Artist's Table

A Cookbook by Master Chefs Inspired by Paintings in the National Gallery of Art

Edited and Compiled by Carol Eron

CollinsPublishersSanFrancisco

A Division of HarperCollins*Publishers*

CONTENTS

INTRODUCTION

Food and the rituals that surround it—from hunting and gathering to harvest and feasting—have long been celebrated in art. This joyful tradition suggested the idea of bringing together paintings and prints from the National Gallery of Art with contemporary masters of the culinary arts. What might one savor at Pierre Bonnard's radiant garden table or in Vincent van Gogh's olive orchard? What do Henri de Toulouse-Lautrec's lady and gentleman pack into their picnic basket for an expedition to the country?

The twelve works of art selected as centerpieces for the menus—ten paintings and two prints—range from the Renaissance to modern times, though the French impressionists and postimpressionists predominate, reflecting the legendary French passion for the culinary arts. Many additional illustrations drawn from the collections of the National Gallery of Art include works by Constable, Manet, Morisot, Renoir, Monet, Pissarro, Cézanne, Gauguin, Homer, Vuillard, Braque, and Picasso. Among these is Jan Steen's amusing Dancing Couple, *which concerns various appetites but nonetheless captures a festive Dutch banquet table, and an enormous mound of butter, by Antoine Vollon, recalling Renoir's sentiment that butter should not be bought packaged but fresh from a creamery.*

The culinary artists—twelve American, one Italian, and one French—were chosen to represent a spectrum of American contemporary cuisine, with homage to its French and Italian legacies. The repasts created in honor of the works of art are not historical renditions with the amplitude of bygone times, but have been designed with contemporary eating and cooking habits in mind. The menus progress from daytime meals through afternoon tea to informal and formal dinners, with two menus for lavish occasions, and conclude with an all-American celebration of dessert.

That said, it should also be said that a lunch might be enjoyed at midnight, and a dinner such as that for A Corner of the Moulin de la Galette *could be served at midday, in honor of Henri de Toulouse-Lautrec's preference for luncheons. The artist believed that guests could enjoy his own culinary celebrations, often whimsical affairs that included food, drink, and entertainment, better at midday than in the evening when they would be tired from working.*

We begin with a picnic in the country, Partie de campagne, *by Toulouse-Lautrec. The lady and gentleman in the carriage, Julia Child imagines, are on their way to meet good friends for an afternoon of convivial feasting in the open air. In their baskets they bring savories, sweets, and wines.*

Roaming in Camille Pissarro's lush kitchen garden, The Artist's Garden at Eragny, *Deborah Madison lets the garden dictate the*

Joseph Decker, *Green Plums* (c. 1885)

Georges Braque, *Still Life: Le Jour* (1929)

menu for an early-springtime luncheon. Pumpkins, *by American artist Walt Kuhn, evokes thoughts of rural Mexican gardens for Rick Bayless, who offers an earthy, rustic meal that reflects the elemental intertwining of pumpkin vines and cornstalks found in these gardens.* Pierre Bonnard's Table Set in a Garden, *with its luminous interplay of light and shadow, provides Jeremiah Tower inspiration for a grand, leisurely luncheon in the French style.*

Mary Cassatt is honored by Marion Cunningham with a tea that, like Cassatt's depiction of the two women in Afternoon Tea Party, is intimate, domestic, and subtle in coloration.

In Still Life with Apples on a Pink Tablecloth, *Paula Wolfert sees a table beckoning to be filled, and Matisse's delight in the delicate yellow-gold of the apples is reflected in her surprising finale.* Matisse's Palm Leaf, Tangier, *one of several garden paintings the* artist made in Morocco in 1912, was painted in a creative burst, the artist said, "tout d'un coup, comme une flamme." What might Monsieur Matisse have enjoyed after a day of painting in the tropics? A light, informal supper, Susan Feniger and Mary Sue Milliken propose, with bursts of intense flavor and color.

With its limpid autumnal light, Still Life with Game, by Jean Siméon Chardin, inspired Patrick Clark to create a menu of muted browns and creams and the bounty of the hunt. Alice Waters responds to the textures and tonalities of Vincent van Gogh's Olive Orchard, a canvas that Van Gogh said he had worked at "from memory because I wanted something very far away like a vague memory softened by time." Beginning with the memory of her friend Lulu cooking over an open fire in Provence, Waters composes a menu around bouillabaisse that balances varied textures and Van Gogh's pale greens, yellows, and siennas.

Joël Robuchon and Patricia Wells offer a witty play on words and shapes for Henri de Toulouse-Lautrec's A Corner of the Moulin de la Galette, a masterful study of loneliness and isolation. A favored haunt of the artist on Montmartre in Paris, the café was named for a windmill on the site and for the flat, round pastries called galettes that were served with drinks. Toulouse-Lautrec undoubtedly would have approved of this repast, intended for the

kind of occasion that demands a certain lavishness—though it is not suggested here that goldfish be added to the water carafes, as the artist did, to encourage the drinking of wine. He believed that water ruined the palate, and as for milk, he said, "I will drink milk when cows graze on grapes."

One of the greatest paintings in the National Gallery of Art collections is Giovanni Bellini and Titian's Feast of the Gods. This bacchanal, acclaimed for its visual beauty as well as its subject, depicts the gods eating, drinking, and reveling as Priapus attempts to seduce a sleeping nymph. According to the tale from Ovid, the braying of an ass thwarted the adventure. Recalling Renaissance customs for feasting, when powerful rulers drew inspiration from imperial Rome for their vast banquets, Lorenza de' Medici creates a modern version of such a feast. She evokes the period's sculptural presentation of food as well as the Renaissance taste for game and draws on an all'antica palette of spices.

And last, Wayne Thiebaud's ceremonial, most-American Cakes is paid tribute by Nancy Silverton, who sees Thiebaud as a dream artist for those dessert-lovers who believe a meal should close with something quiet, sweet, and beautiful.

—Carol Eron, National Gallery of Art, Washington, D.C.

Berthe Morisot, *In the Dining Room* (1886)

Henri de Toulouse-Lautrec, *Partie de campagne* (1897)

PARTIE DE CAMPAGNE

JULIA CHILD

I have chosen the Toulouse-Lautrec Partie de campagne *because I know they are going out on a picnic with dear friends, whom they will meet in a chestnut grove a bit ahead of us and to the right. Those friends will have the linens, plates, and silverware, as well as a cool bottle of welcoming Champagne, a bottle or two of Chablis, and a rather light, but fully developed red Burgundy for the cheese.*

Our friends in the carriage have a lovely, very French luncheon folded into white linen napery and packed in two wicker baskets in the bottom of the carriage at the back, facing us. There is a ramekin of fresh osetra caviar and biscuits, as well as an onion tart on puff pastry to accompany the Champagne. The main course is cold roast pheasant with thin slices of Parma ham and ripe figs, and a celery rémoulade on a bed of watercress. A half-dozen beautifully ripe tomatoes will be quartered and dressed on the site.

The cheese course is a perfect, meltingly ripe Epoissés, followed by a cunningly assembled salade de fruits. *Chocolate lace wafers accompany the fruit, as well as small bunches of large, sweetly perfumed green grapes.*

The four good friends will feast slowly and lovingly, lolling on the grass, while the dog lies beside them, now and then thumping his tail when the laughter rises.

A PICNIC MENU

Fresh osetra caviar and biscuits

Onion Tart / *Pissaladière*

Cold Roast Pheasant with
Parma Ham and Fresh Figs

Celery Rémoulade

Ripe tomatoes vinaigrette

Epoissés cheese

Salade de fruits

Chocolate Lace Wafers and
large, sweet green grapes

ONION TART/PISSALADIÈRE

Makes one 10-inch tart; serves 4

Topped with meltingly tender, almost caramelized onions, Parmesan cheese, and anchovies, pissaladière is an unusual accompaniment to caviar and Champagne. It softens the bite of the caviar and complements the sparkle of the wine.

It is a good idea to make several disks of puff pastry at a time. Stack them between sheets of plastic in your freezer, and you will have tart makings always at the ready, since the pastry thaws enough to use in the few minutes required to fix the trimmings.

WINE SUGGESTION
Champagne

2 tablespoons high-quality olive oil
3 1/2 to 4 cups thinly sliced onions (approximately 1 pound)
A good pinch of fresh or dried thyme leaves
Salt and freshly ground white pepper to taste

1 pound chilled homemade or thawed frozen puff pastry (see p. 94)
3 tablespoons freshly grated Parmesan cheese
One 2-ounce, freshly opened can flat anchovy fillets, oil-packed (optional—there are those who do not like anchovies!)

❁ To make the onion topping, set a 10-inch nonstick skillet or sauté pan over medium-low heat and add the olive oil and then the onions. Sauté them slowly, stirring frequently, for 5 to 6 minutes, or until the onions are tender and translucent. Raise the heat to medium high, and stirring almost constantly, let the onions brown nicely and evenly for several minutes more. Season carefully with thyme, salt, and pepper. Remove from the heat and let cool. Set aside.

❁ To make the crust, roll the chilled puff pastry dough into a long rectangle 1/8 inch thick and 10 1/2 inches wide. Using a plate or cake pan as a guide, cut out as many 10-inch disks as possible. Lightly dampen a baking sheet, loosely roll a disk of dough around the rolling pin, and unroll it on the baking sheet. (Store the rest of the disks on a pizza pan between sheets of plastic wrap, slip everything into a plastic bag, along with the leftover dough, and freeze.) Leaving a 1-inch border all around, prick the pastry disk at 1-inch intervals with a fork, going all the way through to the baking sheet. Sprinkle 1 tablespoon of the cheese over the fork-marked disk and spread the onions on top. Strew the remaining 2 tablespoons of the cheese over the onions and, if you like anchovies, arrange them neatly like the spokes of a wheel over the onions and cheese. Crimp the edges of the pastry up over the edge of the filling. (The tart may be prepared in advance up to this point; cover with plastic wrap and refrigerate for several hours or as long as overnight.)

❁ Preheat the oven to 450 degrees F. Bake the tart in the lower third of the oven for 30 to 40 minutes. It is done when the top has browned lightly and, when you gently lift up a section of the pastry, the bottom is brown and crisp.

❁ To serve warm, transfer the tart to a round platter and cut into wedges. To serve at room temperature or on a picnic, transfer the tart to a rack and let cool completely. When cool, transfer to a platter or napkin-lined pizza pan.

Pierre Bonnard, *Stairs in the Artist's Garden* (1942/1944)

Raoul Dufy, *The Basket* (1926)

COLD ROAST PHEASANT
WITH PARMA HAM AND FRESH FIGS

Serves 4

1 *carrot, peeled*

1 *onion*

1 *celery stalk*

5 *tablespoons unsalted butter at room temperature*

1 *young pheasant, 2 ¹/₂ to 3 pounds, cleaned and ready to cook*

Salt and freshly ground black pepper to taste

4 *thin strips fresh pork fatback or blanched thick-sliced bacon strips**

¹/₄ *cup dry (Sercial) Madeira*

4 *ounces Parma ham, thinly sliced, for serving*

12 *ripe fresh figs, if available, for serving*

❋ Dice the carrot, onion, and celery stalk roughly into ¹/₄-inch pieces. Melt 2 tablespoons of the butter in a saucepan over medium heat. Add the diced vegetables and sauté them for 5 to 6 minutes, or until tender. Set aside until needed.

❋ Meanwhile, salt and pepper the cavity of the pheasant and insert 1 tablespoon of the butter. Truss the bird with white cotton string and rub the bird all over with the remaining 2 tablespoons of butter. Choose a covered heatproof casserole just large enough to hold the pheasant comfortably. Set it over medium-high heat and brown the bird by cooking it for several minutes on all sides, turning it carefully. Remove the pheasant from the casserole, salt it, and tie the strips of fatback or bacon over its breast. (All of this may be achieved in the morning, or the day before serving, and the bird covered and refrigerated until needed.)

❋ To roast the pheasant, count on approximately 1 hour (and an extra 20 minutes or so for the bird to rest before carving, if you are to be serving it warm for a dinner at home). Preheat the oven to 350 degrees F. Strew the cooked diced vegetables in the bottom of the casserole, place the pheasant on its side in the casserole, and pour in the Madeira. Heat the casserole briefly on top of the stove, just until it starts to sizzle, then cover it and set it in the lower third of the preheated oven. After 20 minutes, quickly salt the bird very lightly, baste it with the accumulated juices, and turn it on its other side. After another 20 minutes, turn the bird breast up, baste and salt it, and continue the roasting. The pheasant is done when its legs will just move in their sockets, the juices run clear yellow when a thigh is pierced, and the last juices to fall from the vent when the bird is lifted and drained are clear yellow with no rosy tinge. Remove the pheasant from the casserole and let it cool for 20 minutes or so before very carefully removing the trussing strings and fat strips.

❋ If you are to serve it cold, let the pheasant cool to room temperature, then cover and refrigerate it. To serve, carve off the wings and legs, separate the legs from the thighs, and carve the breast into neat slices. Arrange on a platter and surround with the ham and the whole figs.

*To blanch bacon: Cook bacon strips in 4 cups of boiling water for 5 minutes, then drain and dry on paper towels.

This pheasant is roasted in a cocotte with aromatic vegetables and a whisper of Madeira to perfume the flesh. Only a young pheasant can be roasted (an old one must be braised), and one can easily tell youth from age by the state of the breastbone: The tail end of it is still flexible. A good ¹/₄ inch of it is cartilage that has not yet turned into unyielding bone.

WINE SUGGESTION
Chablis

CELERY RÉMOULADE

Makes approximately 4 cups; serves 6 to 8

That big, brown, knobby, ugly vegetable known as celery root or celeriac is almost snowy white inside and makes a marvelous salad or an accompaniment to smoked or broiled fish, cold cuts, and other vegetables. Because celery root can be tough unless it is very finely shredded, you will need either a food processor with a fine shredding disk or a hand-cranked julienne mill.

One 1-pound celery root (3 to 3 $^1/_2$ inches
   in diameter)
1 $^1/_2$ teaspoons salt
1 $^1/_2$ teaspoons fresh lemon juice

DRESSING
$^1/_4$ cup Dijon mustard
3 tablespoons boiling water

$^1/_3$ to $^1/_2$ cup olive or mild vegetable oil
2 to 3 tablespoons white wine vinegar
Salt and freshly ground white pepper to taste
2 to 3 tablespoons minced fresh parsley (optional)
$^1/_3$ to $^1/_2$ cup sour cream (optional)

1 bunch of watercress, stemmed

❋ To prevent the celery root from discoloring, work quickly. Peel the brown outside off the celery root with a short, stout knife, and cut the celery root into 1-inch chunks. Shred in a food processor fitted with a fine shredding disk or in a hand-cranked julienne mill. At once, toss the shredded root in a large bowl with the salt and lemon juice—lemon helps prevent discoloration, and lemon and salt together have a mildly tenderizing effect. (If you are doubling or tripling the recipe, shred and season the root in batches.) Let it steep for 20 minutes.

❋ Meanwhile, to make the dressing, place a large bowl over a pan of simmering water to warm. Set the warm bowl on your work surface, add the mustard, and by dribbles whisk in the boiling water, then the oil; finally, dribble and whisk in the vinegar to make a thick, creamy sauce.

❋ To assemble, rinse the celery root in cold water, drain, and dry it. Fold it into the dressing and correct the seasoning with salt and pepper. If desired, fold in the parsley and enough sour cream to lightly coat the strips. Serve the celery root on a serving plate atop a bed of watercress.

Note: The celery root is ready to serve now, but will be more tender if it steeps, covered, for several hours in the refrigerator—where it will keep nicely for several days.

Claude Monet, *Woman Seated under the Willows* (1880)

Pierre Bonnard, *Bouquet of Flowers* (c. 1926)

CHOCOLATE LACE WAFERS

Makes approximately 2 1/2 dozen 4-inch wafers

4 ounces (1 stick) unsalted butter, cut up
1/4 cup dark unsulphured molasses
1/4 cup packed light brown sugar
1/4 cup heavy (whipping) cream
2 tablespoons white corn syrup
1 teaspoon ground ginger
A big pinch of salt

1 cup cake flour (scooped and leveled), sifted onto
  waxed paper
1/3 cup small semisweet chocolate chips or chopped
  semisweet chocolate

Small bunches of large, sweet green grapes, as an
  accompaniment

These unusual cookies—caramelized, crisply chewy, and chocolatey—are somewhat persnickety to make but worth the trouble.

❈ Preheat the oven to 375 degrees F. Line 2 baking sheets smoothly with wide heavy-duty aluminum foil, shiny side up, tucking the foil in under the edges of the sheets all around; spray with vegetable-oil cooking spray.

❈ Place all the ingredients, except the flour and chocolate, in a 2-quart saucepan over medium heat and bring just to a simmer. Meanwhile, bring a larger saucepan filled with 2 inches of water almost to a simmer. Remove the pan with the butter mixture from the heat and whisk in the flour. Set the smaller pan in the larger pan of not quite simmering water.

❈ Form and bake 4 wafers at a time, placing 1-tablespoon blobs of batter 3 inches apart on one of the prepared baking sheets. Spread the batter out with the back of a spoon into even 2-inch disks. Bake them on the middle shelf of the oven for approximately 3 minutes, or until bubbling. Even the cookies out with the back of a spoon again if necessary before rapidly sprinkling 1/2 teaspoon of the chocolate over each. Bake for 3 to 4 minutes more, or until the bubbling has almost ceased and the cookies have browned nicely. Meanwhile, form another 4 wafers on the second prepared baking sheet.

❈ Remove the baking sheet from the oven and let it cool for 3 minutes, then peel the cookies off the foil and place them on a wire rack to crisp. Repeat until all the cookies are baked, respraying the foil on the still-warm pan for each batch.

❈ Store the wafers in a warming oven until serving time, or let cool and store for several days in an airtight container. Wrapped tightly, they may also be frozen. Serve the wafers with the grapes.

C. Pissarro. 1898

THE ARTIST'S GARDEN AT ERAGNY

DEBORAH MADISON

A woman bends over a row of plants in the artist's garden. Perhaps she is picking salad greens, but she does not seem to have a basket. Maybe she will use her apron, or maybe she just came to see how they are growing. She bends down and pulls a weed, runs her hand through the greens, letting their scents and shapes suggest the menu for lunch. There will be four people. It is an early-summer day, and wind tosses the trees. Roses frame the edge of the garden, undoubtedly hiding low clumps of fraises des bois. Near the woman grow artichokes or cardoons, and this being a French garden, one supposes that shallots, herbs, and a henhouse are also nearby. There must be new potatoes here, too, smaller than hens' eggs, yellow and waxy, for the main course: a braise of baby artichokes with the potatoes and shallots, sitting on a beautiful bed of buttered spinach. But first, a plate of freshly picked radishes, followed by scrambled eggs scented with garden herbs and accompanied with toast. After the stew, a simple salad of red leaves, for contrast with the greenness of the other vegetables. For dessert, a wedge of delicate yeasted cake with a dome of crackling sugar, accompanied by a few wild strawberries and a spoonful of crème fraîche. Wine is enjoyed throughout the meal, and coffee or a tisane of lemon thyme or lemon verbena follows the dessert.

A LUNCHEON MENU

Crudités of Fresh Radishes

Scrambled Eggs with Fines Herbes
and Toast

Artichoke, Shallot, and Potato
Ragoût on a Bed of Spinach

Red Leaf Salad with Walnut Dressing

Yeasted Sugar Cake with *Fraises
des Bois* and Crème Fraîche

Tisane of Lemon Thyme or
Lemon Verbena

Camille Pissarro, *The Artist's
Garden at Eragny* (1898)

CRUDITÉS OF FRESH RADISHES

Serves 4

❀ Rinse the earth off a dozen or so freshly picked radishes, preferably long, mild breakfast radishes, although a variety of radishes will be fine, too. Do not remove their leaves. Place them in a simple white china dish and serve with little bowls of sea salt for dipping.

SCRAMBLED EGGS WITH FINES HERBES AND TOAST

Serves 4

WINE SUGGESTION
Chenin Blanc or rosé

4 *pieces buttered thin toast*

8 *eggs*

2 *tablespoons water*

1 *tablespoon minced fresh tarragon*

1 *tablespoon minced fresh chives*

1 *tablespoon minced fresh chervil*

3 *tablespoons unsalted butter*

*Salt and freshly ground black or white pepper
    to taste*

❀ Just before you prepare the eggs, make the buttered toast, cutting each piece in two. Set them on 4 warmed plates and keep them warm.

❀ Break the eggs into a medium bowl and beat with a whisk, adding the water and herbs. Melt the butter in a 10-inch skillet or sauté pan over medium-low heat. When the butter foams, add the eggs and begin stirring them gently with a wooden spoon. Keep the spoon moving over and through the eggs, scraping it along the bottom of the pan. After 4 minutes or so the eggs should form soft, creamy curds. Remove the eggs from the heat, season with salt and pepper, divide them among the plates, and serve.

Winslow Homer, *Fresh Eggs* (1874)

ARTICHOKE, SHALLOT, AND
POTATO RAGOÛT ON A BED OF SPINACH

Serves 4

Whole baby artichokes end up pleasantly plump and tender in this vegetable ragoût. It is the ingredients that are special— the technique is easy.

16 *baby artichokes*
1/2 *lemon, plus 1 lemon quartered, for garnish*
8 *small Yellow Finn or red potatoes*
12 *large shallots*
2 *small bunches fresh spinach (approximately 10 ounces each)*
1 *tablespoon extra virgin olive oil*
4 *to 6 tablespoons (1/2 to 3/4 stick) unsalted butter*
1 *garlic clove, slivered*

3 *teaspoons minced fresh rosemary*
3 *fresh thyme sprigs*
1 *bay leaf*
Salt and freshly ground pepper to taste
3/4 *cup dry white wine*
1 1/2 *cups water*
4 *teaspoons minced fresh parsley or tarragon, for garnish*

❀ Break the outer leaves off each artichoke until you reach the paler leaves. Do not stint—tough leaves are stringy and unpleasant to eat. Trim the stem, cut 1/2 inch off the top, and rub the cut part with the lemon half. Boil the artichokes for 5 minutes in salted water, then drain them and set aside.

❀ Peel the potatoes using clean, even strokes, and halve or quarter them lengthwise. Separate the shallots where natural divisions occur. If you see any sign of sprouts, slice them in half, keeping the root end intact, and pry them out with a paring knife. Cut the stems off the spinach, sort through the leaves, and remove any that are bruised. Wash the spinach well in 2 changes of water and set it aside.

❀ Heat the oil and 2 tablespoons of the butter in a Dutch oven or sauté pan over medium heat and add the garlic, 2 teaspoons of the rosemary, the thyme sprigs, and bay leaf. Add the artichokes, potatoes, and whole shallots and cook, shaking the pan occasionally, until the potatoes start to color here and there, approximately 5 minutes. Season with salt and pepper, and add the wine. Simmer for 3 to 4 minutes. Lower the heat, add the water, cover the pan, and simmer until the vegetables are tender when pierced with a knife, 15 to 20 minutes.

❀ Just before serving, place the spinach, with the water clinging to its leaves, in a large skillet or sauté pan over medium-high heat. Sprinkle it with salt to taste and cook the spinach, uncovered, until it wilts, turns bright green, and the juices have cooked away. Add the remaining 2 to 4 tablespoons butter, lower the heat, and toss the leaves repeatedly to coat them with the butter. Season with freshly ground pepper.

❀ Divide the spinach among 4 plates, pushing it out toward the edges. Spoon the ragoût in the middle, garnish with the parsley or tarragon and the remaining 1 teaspoon rosemary, and place a wedge of lemon on each plate.

John Constable, *Wivenhoe Park, Essex* (1816)

Camille Pissarro, *Orchard in Bloom, Louveciennes* (1872)

RED LEAF SALAD WITH WALNUT DRESSING

Serves 4

1 *large shallot, minced*
1 *tablespoon red wine vinegar*
$^1/_4$ *teaspoon salt, plus more to taste*
2 *tablespoons sunflower seed oil*
2 *tablespoons walnut oil*

8 *large handfuls mixed red-leaved greens, such as*
   lolla rossa, red romaine (sliced or broken into
   small pieces), Red Sails, tender beet greens
   and baby red chard

❀ Combine the shallot, vinegar, and $^1/_4$ teaspoon salt in a small bowl, mix well, then whisk in the oils. Taste and adjust the balance of oil to vinegar, if needed. Place the greens in a large bowl and toss with a little salt. Add the dressing and toss gently, using your hands, until the leaves are all lightly coated with the dressing. Mound the salad on individual the plates and serve.

YEASTED SUGAR CAKE WITH
FRAISES DES BOIS AND CRÈME FRAÎCHE

Makes one 9-inch single-layer cake; serves 8 to 10

Serve this tender cake with berries, preferably the tiny wild (or cultivated) strawberries called fraises des bois, *with crème fraîche alongside. The sticky dough, almost a batter, is easier to manage in a mixer than by hand. Use leftover cake for toast or bread pudding.*

CAKE

$^1/_4$ *cup warm water*

1 *package (2 $^1/_2$ teaspoons) active dry yeast*

$^1/_4$ *cup granulated sugar*

2 *cups unbleached all-purpose flour*

$^1/_2$ *teaspoon salt*

$^1/_2$ *cup warm (scalded) milk*

2 *eggs at room temperature*

4 *tablespoons ($^1/_2$ stick) unsalted butter at room temperature*

TOPPING AND GARNISH

3 *tablespoons unsalted butter at room temperature*

Approximately $^1/_2$ cup packed light brown sugar

2 *cups fraises des bois or other small, sweet strawberries*

4 *large rose geranium leaves*

$^1/_2$ *cup crème fraîche*

❧ To make the cake, place the warm water in a small bowl and stir in the yeast and 1 teaspoon of the sugar. Let it stand until foamy, approximately 10 minutes. Lightly butter a large bowl and set it aside.

❧ Combine 1 $^3/_4$ cups of the flour, the remaining sugar, and the salt in a medium bowl. Add the yeast mixture to the flour mixture, along with the warm milk and eggs. Mix until well blended with the paddle attachment of an electric mixer set on high or with a wooden spoon, then add the butter and beat vigorously. If using a mixer, reduce the speed. Gradually mix in the remaining flour. Mix for 5 minutes, or until smooth and silky looking, then scrape the batterlike dough into the buttered bowl. Cover and let rise in a warm place until doubled in bulk, approximately 1 hour.

❧ Lightly butter a 9-inch tart pan with a removable bottom. Turn the dough out onto a lightly floured work surface and gently form it into a disk. Set it in the tart pan and flatten it with your hands so that it fills the pan evenly. To add the topping, rub the butter all over the top and then cover evenly with the brown sugar. Set the tart pan on a baking sheet. Cover and let rise for 20 minutes. Meanwhile, preheat the oven to 400 degrees F.

❧ Bake the cake on the middle shelf of the oven for approximately 18 minutes, or until it is well risen and the sugar has begun to melt and brown. Set the cake on a wire rack to cool briefly, then unmold onto a plate.

❧ To serve, lay a rose geranium leaf on each dessert plate and mound the berries on top. (If they are cultivated strawberries, rinse, slice, and lightly sugar them first.) Spoon a little crème fraîche next to each mound of berries and add a slice of the sugar cake. Follow with coffee or a tisane.

Georges Braque, *Peonies* (1926)

TISANE OF LEMON THYME OR LEMON VERBENA

Serves 4

❀ Place approximately 20 large sprigs of lemon thyme or a handful of fresh lemon verbena leaves in a teapot, pour in 4 cups of boiling water, and allow the mixture to steep for several minutes. Strain into cups to serve.

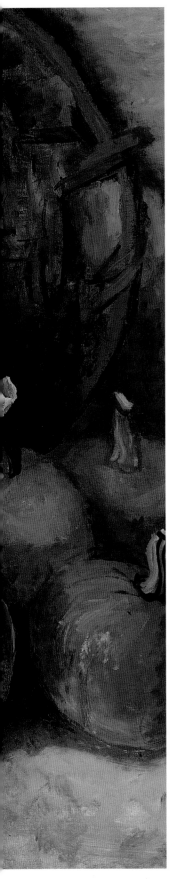

PUMPKINS

RICK BAYLESS

Pumpkins, native to this continent, have sustained cultures here for ages, and they possess a stunningly rustic natural beauty, at once confident and elusive. The markets of Mexico—some of my favorite places on the planet—are filled with scores of pumpkins, from tiny, tender globes to hulking plinths of seaweed green. Each pumpkin has its use, its taste and texture, and each homegrown cornfield has its vines winding wildly up the cornstalks, reconfirming the interconnectedness of these two elements in everyday rural sustenance.

That said, I wanted a menu as homey and elemental as this painting. Immediately I thought of breakfast or brunch, one of the most intimate, relaxed meals I know. I thought of a rustic, homey meal, although one with decidedly contemporary flavors.

A BRUNCH MENU

Jícama Salad with Tangerines
and Cilantro/*Ensalada de Jícama*

Quick-Simmered Tortilla Casserole
with Roasted-Tomatillo Sauce/
Chilaquiles Verdes

Smoky Braised Mexican Pumpkin
with Seared White Onion
and Chipotle Salsa/*Calabaza
Guizada al Chipotle*

Eggs with Mexican Sausage/
Huevos con Chorizo

Prickly Pear Ice/*Nieve de Tuna*

Pot-Brewed Coffee with Raw Sugar
and Spices/*Café de Olla*

Walt Kuhn, *Pumpkins* (1941)

JÍCAMA SALAD WITH TANGERINES AND CILANTRO/
ENSALADA DE JÍCAMA

Serves 4 to 6

If you cannot find the wonderfully bitter Seville oranges for this salad, you can mix your own juice substitute according to the instructions that follow.

1 small (1-pound) jícama, or 1 pound small fresh turnips and/or daikon radishes, peeled and cut into ³/₄-inch cubes

1 cup Seville orange juice or mock Seville orange juice (recipe follows)

¹/₄ teaspoon salt, plus more to taste

1 red-skinned apple, cored and cut into ³/₄-inch cubes (optional)

¹/₂ small cantaloupe, peeled, seeded, and cut into ³/₄-inch cubes (optional)

3 tangerines, peeled, broken into sections, and seeded

Approximately 2 tablespoons roughly chopped fresh cilantro

Approximately 1 teaspoon ground dried chile

2 or 3 small romaine lettuce leaves, for garnish

❁ Place the jícama in a large nonaluminum bowl. Pour in the bitter orange juice and sprinkle with the ¹/₄ teaspoon of salt. Toss well, cover, and let stand at room temperature for 1 hour or so.

❁ Approximately 15 minutes before serving, add the apple and cantaloupe, if desired, and the tangerines and cilantro to the bowl. Mix thoroughly. Toss the mixture every few minutes until serving time. Season the salad with the chile and add more salt and cilantro, if desired. Toss one final time and scoop the salad, along with its juice, into a serving dish lined with the romaine leaves. Drizzle with any orange juice remaining in the bowl and serve.

MOCK SEVILLE ORANGE JUICE

Makes 1 generous cup

6 tablespoons fresh lime juice

³/₄ cup fresh grapefruit juice

¹/₂ teaspoon grated orange zest

❁ Stir together all the ingredients in a nonaluminum bowl, cover, and let stand for 2 to 3 hours. Strain to remove the zest before using. Extra juice should be covered, refrigerated, and used within 24 hours.

Paul Cézanne, *Still Life* (c. 1900)

QUICK-SIMMERED TORTILLA CASSEROLE WITH ROASTED-TOMATILLO SAUCE/CHILAQUILES VERDES

Serves 4 as a side dish; 2 as main course

Chilaquiles, tortillas cooked in a locally popular sauce with an endless variety of meats, vegetables, and cheeses, are a favorite in coffee shops throughout Mexico. After the simmering, the tortillas take on the texture of a coarse polenta. If you can find fresh epazote, a pungent, jagged-leaved herb also known as pigweed, add it to this dish. It is sometimes available in Latin American markets.

6 medium-thick (5 to 6 ounces total) corn tortillas, preferably store-bought and allowed to become stale
$^1/_3$ cup vegetable oil
2 cups Roasted-Tomatillo Sauce (recipe follows)
$^1/_2$ cup chicken broth
$^1/_2$ cup chopped boneless cooked chicken (optional)
1 large fresh epazote sprig (optional)

Approximately $^1/_4$ teaspoon salt
$^1/_4$ cup Thick Cream* (recipe follows) or sour cream thinned with a little milk or cream
2 tablespoons crumbled Mexican cheese, such as queso fresco or queso añejo, or feta, farmer cheese, or mild Parmesan
1 onion slice, separated into rings

❋ Cut the tortillas into eighths. If they are moist, dry them out in a 350-degree-F oven for a few minutes, or until they are quite leathery. Heat the oil in a medium skillet or sauté pan over medium-high heat. When it is almost smoking, or hot enough to make the edge of a tortilla piece sizzle sharply, add half of the tortilla pieces. Turn them frequently until they are lightly browned and nearly crisp, approximately 3 minutes. Remove them with a slotted spoon and drain them on paper towels. Fry and drain the remaining tortilla pieces in the same fashion. Reduce the heat to medium low and discard any oil that remains.

❋ Return the tortilla pieces to the skillet and add the tomatillo sauce, broth, and the chicken and epazote, if desired. Stir well to coat the tortillas, cover the skillet, and simmer until the tortillas are soft but not mushy, approximately 5 minutes. Add the salt to taste.

❋ Scoop the mixture onto a warm serving platter. Drizzle with the thick cream or sour cream, sprinkle with the cheese, and decorate with the onion rings. Serve immediately.

Note: To make larger quantities of the recipe: Fry batches of tortillas in $^1/_2$ inch oil until nearly crisp; drain and place in an 8-inch-square baking dish. Heat together the sauce and broth and pour it over the tortillas, then mix in the chicken and epazote, if desired, and the salt. Cover and bake in a preheated 350-degree-F oven for approximately 20 minutes before topping with the cream, cheese, and onion rings.

*This cream requires 12 to 24 hours to thicken.

THICK CREAM/CREMA ESPESA

Makes 1 cup

1 cup heavy (whipping) cream   *2 teaspoons buttermilk*

❀ Pour the cream into a small saucepan, place it over low heat, and stir just until the chill is off, approximately 1 to 2 minutes; do not heat it above lukewarm (100 degrees F). Stir in the buttermilk and pour into a glass jar.

❀ Set the lid loosely on the jar and place it in a warm (80- to 90-degree-F) spot. Let the cream sit for 12 to 24 hours, or until it becomes noticeably thicker, almost like yogurt or sour cream. Stir it gently, tighten the lid, and refrigerate for at least 4 hours to chill and complete the thickening. The cream will keep for 1 1/2 weeks, covered and refrigerated.

ROASTED-TOMATILLO SAUCE/SALSA VERDE ASADO

Makes approximately 2 cups

1 pound (approximately 11) fresh tomatillos,   *1 large garlic clove, roughly chopped*
*   husked*   *1 tablespoon lard or vegetable oil*
3 fresh serrano or 2 jalapeño chiles, stemmed   *2 cups chicken or beef broth*
5 or 6 fresh cilantro sprigs, roughly chopped   *Approximately 1/2 teaspoon salt (depending on the*
1 small onion, chopped   *   saltiness of the broth)*

❀ Place the tomatillos in a medium cast-iron skillet over medium heat and cook, turning them occasionally, for approximately 10 minutes, or until they are soft and browned. Place the tomatillos and chiles in a blender along with the cilantro, onion, and garlic; stir well. Purée until almost smooth; a little texture should remain.

❀ Heat the lard or vegetable oil in a medium-large skillet over medium-high heat. When hot enough to make a drop of the purée sizzle sharply, pour the purée in all at once and stir constantly for 4 or 5 minutes, or until it has darkened and thickened. Add the broth, let the sauce return to a boil, reduce the heat to medium, and simmer uncovered until the sauce is thick enough to coat a spoon, approximately 10 minutes. Season with salt.

SMOKY BRAISED MEXICAN PUMPKIN WITH SEARED WHITE ONION AND CHIPOTLE SALSA/ CALABAZA GUIZADA AL CHIPOTLE

Serves 4 as a light entrée, or 6 as a hearty side dish

This can also be served with rice for a light entrée, or as a side dish for a sauceless main course such as roasted or grilled poultry.

BRAISING SAUCE

6 Roma (plum) tomatoes (approximately
   12 ounces total)
1 tablespoon good-tasting pork lard or olive oil
8 ounces lean boneless pork shoulder, cut into
   $^1/_2$-inch pieces
One 6-ounce white onion, thinly sliced

Chipotle Salsa (recipe follows)
$^1/_4$ cup chicken broth or water
$^1/_2$ teaspoon salt or to taste

4 cups $^3/_4$-inch-diced Mexican pumpkin, sugar
   pumpkin, or Hubbard or butternut squash
   (approximately 2 pounds before peeling and
   seeding)

❋ To make the braising sauce, preheat the broiler. Place the tomatoes on a broiler pan or baking sheet and broil them 4 inches from the heating element until they are blackened, approximately 4 minutes. Turn over the tomatoes and broil the other side. Remove from the broiler, let cool, and then peel off the blackened skin. Cut out the core and coarsely chop the tomatoes.

❋ In a heavy 12-inch skillet (preferably cast iron), heat the lard or oil over medium-high heat. Add the cubed pork, and fry, stirring and scraping up bits of the browned meat, until it is nicely golden, approximately 10 minutes. Using a slotted spoon, transfer the meat to a small bowl, leaving behind as much oil as possible.

❋ Add the onion to the same skillet and fry, over medium-high heat, stirring regularly, until it is well browned, approximately 10 to 12 minutes. Add the chipotle salsa and tomatoes to the skillet and cook for several minutes, stirring, until the mixture has reduced and thickened. Stir in the broth or water and the salt.

❋ Approximately 1 hour before serving, preheat the oven to 400 degrees F. Place the pieces of pumpkin or squash in an ovenproof baking-serving dish just large enough to hold them in a layer 1 $^1/_4$-inches deep (a 9-inch-square Pyrex dish works well). Mix in the pork and pour the braising sauce over the mixture. Cover with aluminum foil or a lid and bake in the oven for 40 to 45 minutes, or until the pumpkin or squash is just tender. Uncover the dish, raise the oven temperature to 400 degrees F, and bake until the sauce has reduced a little and the top is browned and crusty, approximately 15 minutes.

George Catlin, *Green Corn Dance—Minatarrees,* detail (1861)

CHIPOTLE SALSA/SALSA PICANTE DE CHILE CHIPOTLE

Makes approximately 1 ¹/₄ cups

3 to 6 *dried chiles chipotles colorados (chiles moritos),*
    2 to 4 *dried chiles chipotles mecos, or 3 to 6*
    canned chiles chipotles en adobo
Boiling water, as needed

3 *large garlic cloves, unpeeled*
5 *tomatillos (approximately 8 ounces), husked*
¹/₂ *teaspoon salt or to taste*
¹/₄ *teaspoon granulated sugar or to taste (optional)*

Chipotles colorados (chiles moritos) will give the salsa the cleanest flavor with a deep reddish color and a nice balance. The chipotles mecos are extremely smoky and hot and lacking in the dried-fruit sweetness of the colorados. The canned chipotles en adobo will add a noticeable vinegar and tomato flavor to the finished salsa.

❈ If using dried chiles, break off the stems. Heat a dry, heavy skillet or griddle over medium heat. Place the chiles, a few at a time, on the hot surface and press them flat with a metal spatula for a few seconds, or until they start to crackle and even send up a faint wisp of smoke. Then turn them and press down to toast the other side. Transfer the toasted chiles to a medium bowl, cover with boiling water, weight with a plate to submerge them, and let soak for 20 minutes. Drain and set aside. If using canned chiles, simply remove the chipotles from the adobo sauce they are packed in and set aside.

❈ Heat the same skillet or griddle over medium heat and toast the garlic cloves, turning them occasionally, until they are blackened in spots and soft, approximately 10 to 15 minutes. Let cool, and then slip off the papery skins. Coarsely chop the garlic.

❈ Preheat the broiler. Place the tomatillos on a broiler pan or baking sheet lined with aluminum foil and broil them approximately 4 inches from the heating element for approximately 5 minutes, or until they are blistered and dark. Turn the tomatillos and broil them for another 5 minutes or so until blistered and dark on the second side. Let cool completely.

❈ Place the tomatillos and any juice that has accumulated around them in a blender or in a food processor fitted with the steel blade. Add the chiles and garlic. Blend to a fairly smooth purée. Transfer the mixture to a bowl and stir in enough water to give the salsa a medium consistency. Add salt and if you want to soften the tangy edge, a little sugar.

Marc Chagall, *The Hen with the Golden Eggs* (1927/1930)

EGGS WITH MEXICAN SAUSAGE/
HUEVOS CON CHORIZO

Serves 4

1 *tablespoon vegetable oil, plus more if needed*
8 *ounces chorizo sausage, removed from casings*
    (approximately 1 cup, crumbled)
1 *small onion, chopped (optional)*

1 *medium-large ripe tomato, cored and chopped*
    (optional)
8 *large eggs*
Approximately $^1/_2$ teaspoon salt (or less if the
    chorizo is very salty)

❀ Heat 1 tablespoon oil in a medium skillet or sauté pan over medium-low heat, add the chorizo and cook, stirring occasionally to break up the clumps, until it is browned, approximately 10 minutes. Remove the chorizo with a slotted spoon, then discard all but approximately 2 tablespoons of fat from the skillet (or add vegetable oil to bring it to that quantity). Add the onion and the tomato, if desired, and cook, stirring frequently, until the onion begins to soften and/or the tomato is soft, approximately 7 minutes. Return the chorizo to the pan.

❀ Quickly beat the eggs with the salt in a bowl just to combine the whites and yolks. Pour the eggs into the skillet and scramble until they are done to your liking. Taste for salt, then scoop the eggs into a warm dish and serve quickly.

PRICKLY PEAR ICE/NIEVE DE TUNA

Makes 5 to 6 cups

This bright, crimson ice is made from the fruit of the prickly pear, which is available almost year-round in Latin American and southwestern markets.

3 1/2 *pounds (approximately 18 medium) fresh prickly pears*
1 *cup water*

1 *cup granulated sugar, plus a little more if necessary*
Approximately 3 tablespoons fresh lime juice

❀ Cut a 1/2-inch slice off both ends of each of the prickly pears, then make a 1/2-inch-deep incision down one side, end to end. Carefully peel off the rind, starting from the incision; the rind is thick and, if ripe, will easily peel away from the central core of fruit. Roughly chop the peeled prickly pears.

❀ Place the fruit in a blender, add all of the remaining ingredients, and blend for several minutes, or until the sugar is dissolved. Strain through a medium-meshed sieve and taste for sweetness and tartness, adding more sugar or lime juice as necessary. If time permits, refrigerate to chill thoroughly.

❀ Freeze the mixture in an ice cream maker according to the manufacturer's instructions. When the ice comes from the machine, it may be rather soft; for a firmer texture, let it "ripen" in your freezer for a couple of hours before serving.

POT-BREWED COFFEE WITH RAW SUGAR AND SPICES/CAFÉ DE OLLA

Serves 4 to 5

Piloncillo sugar is a cone-shaped cake of pressed, unrefined, dark brown sugar imported from Mexico. It can be found in most Latin American markets.

4 *cups water*
4 *ounces piloncillo sugar, roughly chopped, or* 1/2 *cup packed brown sugar, plus 1 teaspoon molasses*

One 2-inch piece cinnamon stick
A few aniseeds (optional)
2/3 *cup (2 ounces) ground Viennese-roast coffee (medium to coarse grind)*

❀ Place the water, sugar, cinnamon, and the aniseeds, if desired, in a medium saucepan over medium-low heat. Bring the mixture slowly to a boil, stirring to melt the sugar. Stir in the coffee, remove from heat, cover, and let steep for 5 minutes. Strain the coffee through a fine-meshed sieve into cups or mugs and serve immediately.

Edouard Vuillard, *Two Women Drinking Coffee* (c. 1893)

TABLE SET IN A GARDEN
JEREMIAH TOWER

I first saw Bonnard at an exhibition in London in the mid-1960s. The exhibition placed Bonnard back in the limelight after some decades in the shadows of more currently fashionable painters and showed what a brilliant modern artist he was. Although the show was successful, I was somehow there alone in a gallery with the paintings, the guards, and the actor James Fox, then at the peak of his career. I was, after a brief and highly touted painting career (at school), awed by Bonnard, who colored shadows and who saw light everywhere. That day was one of the most important in my life, and I remember it vividly. The outdoor scenes stirred various appetites, and I remember being very hungry and going out to lunch near Green Park with Mr. Fox.

My inspirations for this luncheon are Bonnard, a déjeuner sur l'herbe with Richard Olney in the south of France, and a dinner I cooked for Julia Child, Sybil Bedford, and Simone Beck on a country garden terrace near Marseilles.

A LUNCHEON MENU

＋━━ ⊯◈⊯ ━━＋

Platter of Aged Country Sausage,
Marinated Olives, and
Rosemary Bread Sticks

Grand Shellfish Platter with
Saffron Mayonnaise

Sea Bass Grilled over Vine Cuttings
with Sea Bass Roe Sauce

French and California fresh
and aged goat cheeses

Pear, Apple, and Quince Tarte Tatin
with Jamaican-Pepper Cream

Pierre Bonnard,
Table Set in a Garden (c. 1908)

Edouard Manet, *The Plum* (c. 1877)

PLATTER OF AGED COUNTRY SAUSAGE, MARINATED OLIVES, AND ROSEMARY BREAD STICKS

Serves 6

1 *pound oil-cured green olives*
1 *pound black Seville-style olives*
1 1/2 *cups olive oil*
10 *garlic cloves, unpeeled*
1/3 *cup fresh thyme sprigs*

1/4 *cup small dried red chile peppers*
4 *bay leaves*
15 *strips of orange zest*
6 *aged dry country sausages, thinly sliced*
Rosemary Bread Sticks (recipe follows)

WINE SUGGESTION
*An Italian sparkling wine,
such as Bellavista Franciacorta*

❋ In a large container, place the green and black olives in the olive oil; add the unpeeled garlic cloves, fresh thyme sprigs, red chiles, bay leaves, and orange zest strips. Cover and marinate at room temperature for 5 days. Lift out the olives with a slotted spoon and place on a platter. Arrange the thinly sliced sausage alongside and accompany with Rosemary Bread Sticks.

ROSEMARY BREAD STICKS

Makes approximately 16 bread sticks

1 1/4 *cups warm (105 degrees F) water*
1 *package (2 1/2 teaspoons) active dry yeast*
1/2 *cup olive oil*
1 *teaspoon salt*

1/4 *cup minced fresh rosemary*
Approximately 4 cups bread flour
Kosher salt for sprinkling

❋ Place the water in a large bowl and stir in the yeast. Let sit for approximately 10 minutes, or until foamy. Stir in the oil and salt, and then mix in the rosemary. Stir in the flour, 1/2 cup at time, until the dough pulls away from the side of the bowl. Turn out the dough on a lightly floured work surface and knead for 15 to 20 minutes, or until it is smooth and elastic. Place the dough in a plastic bag, close it tightly, and refrigerate for 1 hour.

❋ Preheat the oven to 300 degrees F. Oil 1 or 2 baking sheets. Cut off 1/4-cup portions of the dough and, using your palms, roll them into 18-inch-long sticks on a lightly floured surface. Place the bread sticks 2 inches apart on the prepared baking sheets and bake them in the oven for 20 minutes, or until firm. Sprinkle the bread sticks with kosher salt, then transfer them to racks to cool.

Edouard Manet, *Oysters* (1862)

GRAND SHELLFISH PLATTER WITH
SAFFRON MAYONNAISE

Serves 6

12 *New Zealand langoustines or jumbo shrimp,*
   in the shell
1 *Dungeness crab, or 12 blue crabs*
12 *pourpres or mussels, in the shell*
1 *pound periwinkles*

18 *oysters in the shell*
Crushed ice
Saffron Mayonnaise (recipe follows)
Lemon wedges, for garnish

❋ Cook the langoustines in a 1-gallon stockpot of boiling salted water for 5 minutes. The shrimp, if using, should be boiled in salted water for 3 minutes, or until they turn pink, and the crabs for 15 minutes (8 minutes if using blue crabs). Scrub the pourpres or mussels well and debeard the mussels, if using. Cook the periwinkles and pourpres or mussels in boiling salted water for 5 minutes. Open the oysters. Let the cooked shellfish cool.

❋ Arrange all the shellfish on a large round platter mounded with crushed ice. Place the saffron mayonnaise in a bowl in the center and garnish with lemon wedges.

SAFFRON MAYONNAISE

Makes approximately 2 cups

2 *large egg yolks*
Juice of 1 *lemon*
6 *saffron threads*

A pinch of salt and freshly ground white pepper
2 *cups French extra virgin olive oil*

❋ Place the egg yolks, lemon juice, saffron, salt, and pepper in a medium bowl and whisk for 1 minute. Begin whisking the oil into the egg mixture, a few drops at a time, until it emulsifies. Continue to whisk in the oil in a fine stream until a thick mayonnaise is formed. Taste and adjust the seasoning.

If you are unable to acquire superb New Zealand langoustines, substitute large shrimp. The pourpres are eaten only in the south of France, around Toulon, and are so bizarre they have no substitutes. But they are the best taste of the ocean I know.

WINE SUGGESTION
A Bandol Rosé, such as Domaine Tempier, or a Chenin Blanc, such as Chappellet Old Vines

SEA BASS GRILLED OVER VINE CUTTINGS
WITH SEA BASS ROE SAUCE

Serves 6

I prefer to use striped sea bass, but many other fish and roes will work, including porgy or sea bream, blue fish, large mackerels, or any red snapper or Pacific snapper.

WINE SUGGESTION
A mature, oaky Chardonnay, such as Carneros Chardonnay Reserve, Robert Mondavi Winery

One 5-pound whole sea bass with roe
    (approximately $1/2$ pound)
1 lemon, juiced (reserve the flesh)
$1/4$ cup mild olive oil
Salt and freshly ground black pepper to taste

4 fresh thyme sprigs
A small bundle of dried vine cuttings (optional)
1 cup rich fish stock
$1/2$ cup extra virgin olive oil
Lemon wedges and parsley sprigs, for garnish

❊ Light a wood or charcoal fire in a grill. Wash the fish under cold water and pat it dry with paper towels. Pour lemon juice over the entire fish and rub the lemon pieces in the cavity. Rub the fish with the mild olive oil, sprinkle with salt and pepper, and place the thyme sprigs in the cavity.

❊ When the coals are medium hot, lay the dried vine cuttings, if you have them, on the coals. When the vine cuttings have turned to coals, place an oiled cooking rack 4 to 6 inches from the coals, let it heat for 2 minutes, and place the fish on the rack. Cook the fish on one side for 10 minutes, then turn and cook it 10 minutes longer, or until the backbone (inside the cavity) is no longer pink.

❊ Meanwhile, place the fish stock in a small pan, bring to a simmer, add the roe, and poach it for 5 minutes. Quickly place the roe and stock in a blender and purée until smooth. Pour the mixture into a medium bowl and whisk in the extra virgin olive oil.

❊ Transfer the fish to a warmed platter and pour the warm sauce over it. Garnish with lemon wedges and parsley and serve.

Childe Hassam, *Oyster Sloop, Cos Cob* (1902)

Charles V. Bond, *Still Life: Fruit, Bird, and Dwarf Pear Tree* (1856)

PEAR, APPLE, AND QUINCE TARTE TATIN
WITH JAMAICAN-PEPPER CREAM

Serves 6

2 *cups granulated sugar*
3 *Bosc pears, halved*
3 *green apples, halved*
3 *ripe quinces, halved*

2 *tablespoons unsalted butter*
A pinch of salt
One unbaked single-crust pastry dough
Jamaican-Pepper Cream (recipe follows)

❊ Preheat the oven to 200 degrees F. Place 1 cup of the sugar in an ovenproof dish that will hold all the fruit in a single layer and place the fruit, cut side down, on top. Bake the fruit for 30 minutes, or until each piece is half-cooked (test with a knife); remove each piece with a slotted spoon as soon as it is ready and set it aside to cool until all the pieces are finished. Peel and core each piece of fruit.

❊ Raise the oven temperature to 375 degrees F. Grease a 12-inch nonstick ovenproof skillet or sauté pan with butter and sprinkle it with the remaining 1 cup sugar. Arrange alternating pieces of pear, apple, and quince in circles, cut-side down, in the pan and sprinkle with the salt. Roll out the pastry on a lightly floured board into a round slightly smaller than the pan's diameter. Roll the pastry around the rolling pin, transfer it to the pan, and carefully lay it over the fruit. Bake the tart for approximately 30 minutes, or until the fruit is tender and the crust is browned.

❊ Remove the tart from the oven and place it on the stove top over medium heat, constantly shaking the pan gently from side to side, until the juices turn light brown, approximately 10 minutes. Let the tart cool for 5 minutes. Place a serving platter on top of the tart pan and invert the platter and tart together, unmolding the tart. Let the tart cool for another 15 minutes, then serve it with the pepper cream.

JAMAICAN-PEPPER CREAM

Makes 1 1/2 cups

2 *teaspoons freshly ground Jamaican or Tellicherry*
   black pepper
1/3 *teaspoon Jamaican vanilla extract, or*
   Madagascar bourbon vanilla extract

1 1/2 *cups crème fraîche or sour cream*
Salt to taste

❊ Mix all the ingredients together well in a medium bowl, cover, and refrigerate for 1 hour before serving. Extra cream can be covered and stored in the refrigerator for several days.

Tarte Tatin is traditionally made with apples, but here the technique is adapted to make a tart of mixed fruit. The pepper cream intensifies and complements the perfume of the fruit.

BEVERAGE SUGGESTIONS
A late-harvest Riesling such as Far Niente "Dolce"
Graffeo coffee
Lapsang Souchong tea
Sandeman 20-year tawny port
Aged Scotch whisky
Old Barbados rum

Mary Cassatt, *Afternoon Tea Party* (1890/1891)

AFTERNOON TEA PARTY
MARION CUNNINGHAM

Mary Cassatt's Afternoon Tea Party *lovingly depicts the luxury of gathering with friends to share talk and tea. I wish we could return more often to such deeply satisfying rituals as this.*

A TEA MENU

Spiced Walnuts

Small Biscuits with Ham

Ginger Shortbread with
Green Mango Fool

Lemon Pound Cake

Crumpets with Peach-Rose Jam

Earl Grey and herbal teas

SPICED WALNUTS

Makes 2 ¹/₂ cups

2 ¹/₂ *cups (10 ounces) walnut halves or large pieces*
1 *cup granulated sugar*
¹/₂ *cup water*

1 *teaspoon ground cinnamon*
1 *teaspoon salt*
1 *tablespoon vanilla extract (optional)*

❀ Preheat the oven to 350 degrees F. Spread the walnuts in one layer on a rimmed baking sheet. Toast in the oven for 10 to 15 minutes (watch carefully—nuts scorch easily), or until the nuts are lightly browned.

❀ Place the sugar, water, cinnamon, and salt in a heavy, medium saucepan. Cook the mixture over medium heat, without stirring, for approximately 10 minutes. The bubbles will become smaller and more compact as the syrup cooks. The syrup is done when it reaches the soft-ball stage (236 degrees F on a candy thermometer or when a small amount of syrup dropped into cold water forms a soft ball that can be picked up).

❀ Remove from the heat, stir in the vanilla, if using, and add the walnuts. Stir the mixture slowly and gently, or until it is creamy. Lightly butter a platter. Pour the nut mixture out onto the prepared platter and separate the walnuts. Let cool. Store any leftover nuts in an airtight container.

Henri Fantin-Latour, *Still Life* (1866)

Gerrit Willemsz. Heda, *Still Life with Ham*, detail (1650)

SMALL BISCUITS WITH HAM

Makes 32 small sandwiches

BISCUITS
2 *cups unbleached all-purpose flour*
1 *tablespoon granulated sugar*
$^1/_2$ *teaspoon salt*
4 *teaspoons baking powder*
$^1/_2$ *cup vegetable shortening*
$^2/_3$ *cup milk*

$^1/_2$ *cup (1 stick) unsalted butter at*
    room temperature
8 *ounces thinly sliced cooked ham*
3 *tablespoons prepared mustard, preferably*
    Dijon-style

❄ To make the biscuits, preheat the oven to 425 degrees F. Grease a baking sheet. Put the flour, sugar, salt, and baking powder in a medium bowl. Cut the shortening into the flour with two knives or a pastry blender until the mixture resembles coarse meal. Add the milk all at once and stir just until the dough forms a ball around the spoon. Turn out the dough onto a lightly floured board and knead 14 times.

❄ On a lightly floured surface, roll out the biscuit dough to a $^1/_4$-inch thickness and cut into rounds with a 1-inch cookie cutter. Place the rounds 1 inch apart on the prepared baking sheet and bake in the oven for 8 to 10 minutes, or until golden.

❄ While they are still warm, split the biscuits and generously butter the insides. Cut the ham to fit the biscuits and place 2 slices, with a dab of mustard, between each 2 halves. Close the sandwiches and serve them warm.

GINGER SHORTBREAD WITH GREEN MANGO FOOL

Makes 24 wedges of shortbread

2 cups unbleached all-purpose flour
1 cup packed dark brown sugar
2 tablespoons ground ginger

1 teaspoon baking soda
1 cup (2 sticks) unsalted butter at room temperature
Green Mango Fool (recipe follows)

❀ Preheat the oven to 325 degrees F. In a large bowl, stir together the flour, brown sugar, ginger, and baking soda until thoroughly mixed. Cut the butter into $1/2$-tablespoon pieces and drop them into the bowl. Blend the butter into the dry ingredients, using your fingertips or a pastry blender, as you would mix a pie dough, until the mixture is crumbly and you see no unblended pieces of butter.

❀ Divide the dough in half and press each piece evenly into each of two 8-inch round cake pans. Prick each shortbread all over with a fork at $1/2$-inch intervals. Bake in the oven for 40 to 45 minutes, or until lightly browned around the edges; the center will stay low, and only the sides will rise slightly.

❀ Let cool for a minute or two, then cut each shortbread into 12 pie-shaped wedges. Remove the wedges from the pans and set on wire racks until cool completely, approximately 30 minutes. To serve, spoon a little mound of mango fool on top of each shortbread wedge. Store any leftover shortbread in an airtight container.

This crunchy, buttery cookie has a smooth texture and spicy ginger overtones. The dough is pressed into pans and baked, then cut into wedges while still warm and soft; it will crisp as it cools.

GREEN MANGO FOOL

Makes approximately 2 $1/2$ cups

2 very firm green (unripe) mangoes, peeled, cut
    from pit, and diced
$1/3$ cup granulated sugar, or more if the fruit is
    very tart

$1/3$ cup water
1 cup heavy (whipping) cream
1 $1/2$ tablespoons nonfat dry milk

❀ Place the diced mangoes in a medium saucepan and add the sugar and water. Cook over medium heat, stirring often, for approximately 10 minutes, or until the fruit is soft. Taste and add more sugar if the fruit is too tart. Remove from the heat and mash the mangoes with a fork until they form a coarse purée. If there is extra liquid, drain some off; the mixture should have the texture of applesauce. Let cool.

❀ Put the cream and nonfat dry milk in a deep bowl and whip until the cream holds firm peaks. (The dry milk helps to stabilize the whipped cream.) Fold the mango purée into the whipped cream until blended. If you have any leftover mango fool, cover and store in the refrigerator for up to one day, or freeze it in an ice cream maker—it makes a delicious ice cream.

LEMON POUND CAKE

Makes one 9-by-5-inch loaf cake

Cake flour gives this pound cake an extra-fine crumb and a delicate texture that suits its lemon flavor. Unbleached all-purpose flour also may be used.

1 cup (2 sticks) unsalted butter at room temperature
1 2/3 cups granulated sugar
5 eggs at room temperature

2 cups cake flour
1/2 teaspoon salt
2 teaspoons grated lemon zest

❋ Preheat the oven to 325 degrees F. Grease and flour a 9-by-5-inch loaf pan. Place the butter in a large bowl and beat until it is creamy. Gradually add the sugar while beating constantly until the mixture is well blended. Add the eggs, one at a time, beating well after each addition. Add the flour and salt and beat until smooth and thoroughly blended. Add the lemon zest and beat another few seconds.

❋ Pour the batter into the prepared loaf pan and smooth the top with a spatula. Bake for approximately 1 hour, or until a toothpick inserted into the center of the cake comes out clean. Let cool in the pan for 5 minutes before turning out onto a rack to cool completely.

Edouard Vuillard, *Woman in a Striped Dress* (1895)

Wagguno, *Fruit and Baltimore Oriole* (1858)

CRUMPETS WITH PEACH-ROSE JAM

Makes 1 dozen 3-inch crumpets

1 package (2 ¹/₂ teaspoons) active dry yeast
¹/₂ cup warm water
1 teaspoon granulated sugar
1 ¹/₂ cups warm milk
2 cups unbleached all-purpose flour

1 teaspoon salt
¹/₂ teaspoon baking soda
Unsalted butter at room temperature, for
    greasing rings
Peach-Rose Jam (recipe follows)

Good crumpets are spongy in texture and are best eaten with jam or butter and honey.

❋ Sprinkle the yeast over ¹/₄ cup of the warm water in a medium bowl. Add the sugar, stir, and let stand for 5 minutes until the yeast dissolves and becomes foamy. Add the milk, flour, and salt. Beat until smooth. Cover the bowl with plastic wrap and let stand for 1 hour (if you want to make the batter the night before, cover and refrigerate overnight).

❋ Stir the batter. Dissolve the baking soda in the remaining ¹/₄ cup warm water and stir into the batter. Cover and let rest for 30 minutes.

❋ Heat a large griddle over medium heat. Grease 12 crumpet rings, each 3 inches in diameter. When the griddle is medium hot, grease it and place the rings on it. Spoon approximately 3 tablespoons of batter into each ring, just enough to cover the bottom. Lower the heat and cook the crumpets for approximately 8 minutes, or until their tops have lost their shine and are filled with little holes. Using pot holders, remove the rings from the griddle, then remove the crumpets from the rings. Repeat to use the rest of the batter and rings, if necessary. Toast the crumpets, butter them generously, and serve them hot with the peach-rose jam alongside.

PEACH-ROSE JAM

Makes approximately 2 cups

2 cups coarsely mashed, peeled and pitted fresh
    peaches (approximately 5 peaches)

Granulated sugar to taste
3 or 4 drops rose water

Rose water is available in many markets, and also in pharmacies, where it is labeled Fluid Rose Soluble. This rose-scented jam is heaven on hot, homemade crumpets.

❋ Put the mashed peaches and sugar in a skillet over low heat and stir the mixture for 1 minute, or just long enough to melt the sugar and blend it with the fruit. Remove from the heat and let cool.

❋ Carefully stir in the rose water to taste; the flavor should be just a shy presence. The jam will keep, covered, for approximately 3 days in the refrigerator.

Henri Matisse, *Palm Leaf, Tangier* (1912)

PALM LEAF, TANGIER

MARY SUE MILLIKEN AND SUSAN FENIGER

We were delighted with the prospect of creating a menu inspired by a painting of the tropics. Matisse's Palm Leaf, Tangier, *evokes a sense of improvisation, an approach we encourage in the kitchen. We both associated this piece with warm weather, tropical ingredients, and light, fresh combinations. The menu we suggest is for a beautiful, balmy evening with friends when you desire small amounts of highly flavored, multi-textured foods and want to sip iced mint tea or a chilled blush wine. We imagine that Matisse might have dined like this after a long day of painting in the tropical gardens of Morocco.*

A SUPPER MENU

Fennel and Sweet Pepper Slaw

Parmesan Orzo with
Yellow Split Pea and Basil Purée

Seared Okra with Chile,
Lime, and Cumin

Milky Date Crunch Ice Cream Balls

FENNEL AND SWEET PEPPER SLAW

Serves 4 to 6

A wonderfully crunchy, vivid salad that has an intriguing flavor and complements almost any pasta.

BEVERAGE SUGGESTION
Iced mint tea

2 *fennel bulbs (approximately 2 pounds)*
2 *red bell peppers*
$^1/_3$ *to* $^1/_2$ *cup extra virgin olive oil*

2 *tablespoons red wine vinegar*
$^1/_2$ *teaspoon sea salt*
5 *to 6 good turns of the peppermill*

❋ Trim the fennel of its feathery leaves and stems and peel off any dry outer parts. Reserve the most tender inner leaves for garnish. Cut the bulbs lengthwise into paper-thin slices and discard the core.

❋ Quarter the bell peppers lengthwise; remove the stems, seeds, and thick white veins. Cut the peppers into very fine, thin julienne and add them to the shredded fennel.

❋ Mix together all the remaining ingredients in a large nonaluminum bowl, whisking to blend. Add the vegetables and toss well. Cover and refrigerate the slaw for at least 30 minutes or for up to half a day.

❋ To serve, roughly chop the reserved fennel leaves and sprinkle on top.

Paul Cézanne, *Still Life with Peppermint Bottle* (c. 1894)

PARMESAN ORZO WITH
YELLOW SPLIT PEA AND BASIL PURÉE

Serves 4 to 6

This is a delightful way to eat pasta. Served with the orzo, the golden split-pea purée with flecks of green makes a dish reminiscent of pasta e fagioli. Leftover purée is great at room temperature spread on toast.

WINE SUGGESTION
A chilled blush wine

1 pound orzo (rice-shaped pasta)
3 tablespoons fine-quality olive oil
¹/₂ cup (2 ounces) finely grated good-quality
    Parmesan cheese

Yellow Split Pea and Basil Purée (recipe follows)

❀ Bring a large pot of salted water to a rolling boil. Add the orzo and stir gently. Cook the orzo for 4 to 7 minutes, or until the pasta is cooked through but firm.

❀ Coat a rimmed baking sheet with a few drops of the olive oil. Drain the orzo in a sieve, shaking off the excess water. Immediately spread the hot orzo out on the tray for 1 to 2 minutes to cool slightly and release as much steam as possible. Scrape the orzo into a large bowl and sprinkle with the remaining olive oil, stirring to coat the pasta. Add the cheese and toss to mix well. Serve immediately with the split-pea purée either atop or alongside the orzo.

YELLOW SPLIT PEA AND BASIL PURÉE

Serves 4 to 6

2 cups dried yellow split peas
5 ¹/₂ cups water
¹/₂ cup olive oil
2 large onions, cut into ¹/₄-inch dice
2 ¹/₂ teaspoons sea salt

³/₄ teaspoon freshly ground black pepper
5 to 6 large garlic cloves, minced
3 large bunches fresh basil, stemmed and
    leaves julienned

❀ Bring the peas and water to a boil in a large, heavy pot. Cover, reduce the heat, and simmer for 1 to 1 ¹/₂ hours, or until the peas become a thick purée.

❀ In another large, heavy pot, heat the olive oil over medium heat. Add the onions, salt, and pepper. Cook gently, stirring occasionally, for 10 to 15 minutes, or until the onions are soft and beginning to turn golden. Add the garlic and sauté, stirring, for 1 to 2 minutes more. Add the peas and simmer for 10 to 15 minutes to blend the flavors. Just before serving, stir in the julienned basil.

Paul Gauguin, *Self-Portrait* (1889)

SEARED OKRA WITH CHILE, LIME, AND CUMIN

Serves 6

1 *pound fresh okra*

¹/₃ *to* ¹/₂ *cup olive oil*

3 *serrano chiles, stemmed, seeded, and minced*

2 *teaspoons ground cumin*

¹/₂ *teaspoon salt*

Freshly ground black pepper to taste

Juice of 1 lime

We chose this dish as a crunchy, sour, and spicy foil to the creaminess of the orzo and peas.

❧ Trim the stems from the okra and cut each pod into 3 pieces on the diagonal. Heat one-third of the olive oil in a 9-inch skillet or sauté pan over high heat until the oil is smoking. Add one-third of the okra and sauté, shaking the skillet, until the okra is slightly browned, approximately 2 to 3 minutes. Using a slotted spoon, transfer the cooked okra to a plate and repeat the process with the remaining okra and olive oil, one-third of each at a time.

❧ When all the okra is cooked, return it to the pan and add the chiles, cumin, salt, and pepper. Cook for approximately 1 minute, stirring occasionally. Sprinkle on the lime juice and serve immediately.

MILKY DATE CRUNCH ICE CREAM BALLS

Serves 6 to 8

2 *cups rolled (old-fashioned) oats*

1 *cup (5 ¹/₂ ounces) natural (unpeeled) almonds,*
   roughly chopped

2 *tablespoons vegetable oil*

2 *tablespoons apple juice*

2 *tablespoons honey*

¹/₈ *teaspoon salt*

2 *cups nonfat milk*

1 *pound fresh dates, preferably Medjool*

3 *cups half-and-half*

6 *egg yolks*

¹/₂ *cup packed brown sugar*

2 *teaspoons vanilla extract*

2 *tablespoons fresh lemon juice*

❊ Preheat the oven to 300 degrees F. Lightly oil a rimmed baking sheet or line it with parchment paper.

❊ Combine the oats and almonds in a medium bowl and mix them together. Place the oil, apple juice, honey, and salt in a shallow pan and warm over low heat, stirring until combined. Pour the liquid over the oats and almonds and toss to coat them well. Spread this mixture on the prepared baking sheet and bake for 30 minutes, stirring occasionally. Remove from the heat and let cool; then transfer the mixture to a small container, cover, and place in the freezer until needed.

❊ Simmer the nonfat milk in a medium saucepan over low heat, stirring often with a wooden spoon, until the milk is reduced to 1 cup; set aside to cool. Remove the pits from the dates and chop the dates into pea-sized pieces. Place half of the date pieces on a plate and set in the freezer. Purée the remaining dates in a blender with the cooled nonfat milk until smooth.

❊ Place the half-and-half in a medium pan over high heat and bring to a full, rolling boil. Meanwhile, whisk the yolks and brown sugar together vigorously in a medium bowl until light in color. As soon as the half-and-half comes to a boil, pour it immediately over the yolk-sugar mixture while whisking. Mix in the date-milk mixture, vanilla, and lemon juice. Cover and refrigerate for 1 to 2 hours.

❊ Freeze the mixture in an ice cream maker according to the manufacturer's instructions. Fold in the reserved frozen date pieces and place in the freezer for 2 to 4 hours more, or until set.

❊ To serve, scoop the ice cream into large round balls, roll them in the oat-almond crunch until they are completely covered, and serve immediately. Or, return the ice cream balls to the freezer for up to one-half day before serving.

Henri Matisse, *Still Life with Pineapple* (1924)

STILL LIFE WITH GAME
PATRICK CLARK

*I love this Chardin—it speaks to me. The light,
the colors, hunting—fall is my favorite season.
I thought of a dinner that would reflect these
harmonies: nutty-tasting sunchoke soup, rabbit
blanketed in earthy vegetables, and a sweet that
balances contrasts of warm and cool, cream,
brown, and green.*

A DINNER MENU

Sunchoke Soup with
Garlic-Rubbed Croutons

Roasted Saddle of Rabbit with
Wild Mushrooms and Parsnips

Warm Chocolate Tarts with
Honey Ice Cream and
Chocolate Tuiles

Jean Siméon Chardin,
Still Life with Game (c. 1760/1765)

SUNCHOKE SOUP WITH GARLIC-RUBBED CROUTONS

Serves 4

Sunchokes, also known as Jerusalem artichokes, are a tuber that resembles ginger root. Since Jerusalem artichokes are not truly artichokes but a variety of sunflower and have nothing to do with Jerusalem, modern growers have begun calling them sunchokes. They have a nutty flavor and almost always leave guests guessing what it is they are eating.

2 pounds sunchokes (Jerusalem artichokes)
3 tablespoons plus 1 teaspoon fresh lemon juice
2 tablespoons unsalted butter
1 large onion, sliced
3 garlic cloves, 2 minced and 1 halved lengthwise
8 cups chicken or vegetable stock
Salt and freshly ground white pepper to taste

12 sourdough baguette slices, each sliced on the diagonal ¹/₂-inch thick
1 ¹/₂ tablespoons vegetable oil
1 ¹/₂ cups heavy (whipping) cream, or half-and-half
2 tablespoons minced fresh chives, for garnish

❋ Peel the sunchokes and cut them into pieces. Place the sunchokes in a bowl of water with the 3 tablespoons lemon juice to prevent discoloration. Melt the butter in a 3-quart stockpot over medium heat. Add the onion, and cook for 7 minutes, or until soft, stirring often. Add the minced garlic and cook for 1 minute more.

❋ Drain the sunchokes and add them to the pot along with the stock. Bring to a boil, then reduce the heat and simmer for approximately 30 minutes, or until the chokes are tender. Season the soup with salt and pepper. Working in batches, transfer the soup to a blender and purée until smooth. Return the soup to the pot.

❋ While the soup is cooking, preheat the oven to 400 degrees F. Place the baguette slices on a baking sheet, brush them with the oil, and bake for 5 minutes, or until they are lightly browned. Rub the oiled side with the garlic clove halves.

❋ Stir the cream and remaining 1 teaspoon lemon juice into the soup. Warm it gently over medium heat, then adjust the seasoning. Serve the soup in shallow bowls, garnished with the chives and the garlic croutons.

Claude Monet, *Jerusalem Artichoke Flowers* (1880)

Jan Steen, *The Dancing Couple* (1663)

ROASTED SADDLE OF RABBIT
WITH WILD MUSHROOMS AND PARSNIPS

Serves 4

MARINADE

1 *cup olive oil*

4 *fresh thyme sprigs*

2 *fresh rosemary sprigs*

4 *fresh sage leaves, crushed*

8 *garlic cloves, crushed*

1 *teaspoon freshly cracked black pepper*

RABBITS AND SAUCE

2 *saddles of rabbit (2 loins, 4 legs)*

$^1/_4$ *cup olive oil*

Salt and freshly ground black pepper to taste

2 *fresh thyme sprigs*

4 *fresh sage leaves*

4 *tablespoons ($^1/_2$ stick) unsalted butter*

2 *shallots, minced*

2 *garlic cloves, minced*

1 $^1/_2$ *cups dry white wine*

2 *cups rabbit or vegetable stock*

2 *teaspoons fresh lemon juice*

MUSHROOMS

$^1/_4$ *cup olive oil*

1 *pound mixed fresh wild mushrooms*

2 *tablespoons unsalted butter*

1 *teaspoon minced fresh thyme*

2 *teaspoons minced shallot*

Salt and freshly ground black pepper to taste

PARSNIPS

4 *large parsnips, peeled and thinly sliced*

2 *tablespoons olive oil*

Salt and freshly ground black pepper to taste

Minced fresh parsley, for garnish

❀ To make the marinade, combine all the ingredients in a nonaluminum bowl large enough to hold the rabbits and mix well. Remove the legs from the saddle. Place the loins and the legs in the marinade, cover, and refrigerate overnight, turning them at least once.

❀ Preheat the oven to 425 degrees F. Remove the meat from the marinade and pat dry with paper towels. Discard the marinade. Heat the olive oil over medium heat in a deep, heavy pot large enough to hold the meat. Season the meat with salt and pepper and place it in the hot pan. Brown the meat on all sides; this should take approximately 3 to 4 minutes. Add the thyme and sage and cover the pot. Place the pot in the oven for 5 minutes. Remove the loins (which cook faster than the legs) and tent them with aluminum foil to keep them warm. Place the pot, with the legs, back in the oven for another 5 minutes. The legs should be done at this point; do not overcook them.

❀ Place the legs with the loins and keep them warm in a low oven. Pour off the excess oil from the pot and add 2 tablespoons of the butter. Add the shallots and sauté for 1 minute. Add the garlic and sauté for 1 more minute. Pour in the wine and cook to reduce it until it is almost completely evaporated. Add the stock and cook until reduced to 1 cup. Stir in the lemon juice and swirl in the remaining 2 tablespoons butter. Season the sauce with salt and pepper, then pass it through a sieve and keep warm.

❀ To cook the mushrooms, heat the oil in a medium skillet or sauté pan over high heat. Add the mushrooms and sauté until their juices are released and have evaporated and the mushrooms have colored a little, approximately 10 minutes. Add the butter, thyme, and shallot and cook 1 minute more. Drain the mushrooms and keep them warm. Season with salt and pepper.

❀ To prepare the parsnips, steam or boil them until they are just tender, approximately 5 to 6 minutes for steaming and 8 minutes for boiling: Be careful not to overcook them. Drain if necessary, and place in a large bowl. Add the olive oil, toss well, and season with salt and pepper.

❀ To serve, make a bed of parsnips on each of 4 plates. Place 1 rabbit leg on each plate. Split each loin across the bone and place one-half beside each leg. Warm the plates for 1 minute in the oven, then divide the mushrooms among the plates and pour the sauce over the rabbit. Sprinkle with the parsley and serve.

WARM CHOCOLATE TARTS WITH
HONEY ICE CREAM AND CHOCOLATE TUILES

Serves 4

HONEY ICE CREAM

8 *egg yolks*

2 ¹/₃ *cups honey*

4 *cups whole milk*

1 *cup plus 2 tablespoons heavy (whipping) cream*

CHOCOLATE TUILES

1 ¹/₄ *cups granulated sugar*

A pinch of salt

1 *cup sifted unbleached all-purpose flour*

¹/₃ *cup unsweetened cocoa powder*

³/₄ *cup egg whites (approximately 6 eggs)*

¹/₂ *cup (1 stick) unsalted butter, melted*

WARM CHOCOLATE TARTS

³/₄ *cup heavy (whipping) cream*

5 *ounces semisweet chocolate, preferably Lindt's*

3 *egg yolks*

1 *tablespoon Kahlúa*

Four 4-inch fluted tart shells (partially baked)

Unsweetened cocoa powder, for dusting

Fresh mint sprigs, for garnish

❧ To make the ice cream, beat the egg yolks and honey together in a large bowl until lemon colored. Bring the milk to a boil in a medium saucepan. Whisk a few spoonfuls of the hot milk into the yolk mixture to temper it, then whisk the yolk mixture into the milk in the saucepan. Cook over low heat, stirring constantly with a wooden spoon, until the mixture thickens and coats the back of a spoon. Remove from the heat and stir in the cream. Strain through a fine-meshed sieve and let cool. Freeze in an ice cream maker according to the manufacturer's instructions.

❧ To make the tuiles, preheat the oven to 325 degrees F. Line 4 baking sheets with parchment paper and spray it lightly with vegetable-oil cooking spray. Place the sugar and salt in a medium bowl; sift the flour and cocoa together into the sugar and stir to blend. Whisk in the egg whites, then whisk in the butter until the batter is smooth.

❧ Spread a thin layer of batter on the prepared baking sheets. Bake for 5 to 7 minutes, or until set and dry-looking. While it is still hot, carefully form the tuiles: Tear large strips of the cookie from the sheet and bend slightly, so that they resemble curved roof tiles. Set them on wire racks to crisp. Leave the oven on to bake the tarts.

❧ To make the tarts, place the cream and chocolate in a medium pan over low heat until they are just warm and the chocolate has melted. Stir in the egg yolks and Kahlúa. Pour the mixture into the tart shells and bake until the custard is set and shiny, approximately 10 to 12 minutes.

❧ To serve, place 1 tart on each of 4 dessert plates. Add a small scoop of honey ice cream and one tuile to each plate. Dust the rims of the plates with cocoa and garnish the dessert with mint sprigs. Serve at once.

Balthasar van der Ast, *Basket of Flowers* (c. 1622)

A CORNER OF THE MOULIN DE LA GALETTE

JOËL ROBUCHON AND PATRICIA WELLS

We have chosen Henri de Toulouse-Lautrec's A Corner of the Moulin de la Galette *because we were immediately inspired by the idea of a meeting place where people gather for good times. We decided to play off the words* moulin, *or mill, and* galette, *which may be any flat, tartlike dish. Thus we offer two galettes—one an appetizer and the other a dessert—and draw upon the* moulin *idea by using a salt crust for a roasted beef tenderloin.*

A DINNER MENU

Truffle, Onion, and Bacon Galettes/
*Galettes de Truffes aux Oignons
et Lard Fumé*

Beef Tenderloin Roasted
in an Herb-Infused Salt Crust/
*Rôti de Filet de Boeuf en
Croûte de Sel aux Herbes*

Field Salad with Fresh Herbs/
Salade aux Herbes Fraîches

Golden Sunburst Apple Galette
with Cinnamon Ice Cream/
*Galette Fine aux Pommes
et Glace à la Canelle*

Henri de Toulouse-Lautrec,
A Corner of the Moulin de la Galette (1892)

TRUFFLE, ONION, AND BACON GALETTES/
GALETTES DE TRUFFES AUX OIGNONS ET LARD FUMÉ

Serves 8

This is a wildly extravagant dish, but there are times and occasions that demand a certain lavishness. Each galette consists of a layer of thinly sliced truffles and a layer of peppery onion, bacon, and cream. If you do not have truffles, the onion mixture is extraordinary as a sort of crustless little onion and bacon tart cooked in ramekins (see p. 85). You would not believe that onions and bacon can taste this good. It is important that the bacon be cut into cubes, which will release a wealth of flavor. If you chill the bacon in the freezer, it will be easier to cut.

WINE SUGGESTION
A great white Burgundy, such as Corton-Charlemagne

8 *fresh black truffles (approximately 1 ¹/₂ ounces each), or substitute 12 ounces canned truffles*
2 *garlic cloves, peeled and halved*
2 *tablespoons unsalted butter, melted*
8 *onions (approximately 2 pounds)*
2 *tablespoons rendered goose fat, or butter*

Sea salt and freshly ground black pepper to taste
8 *very thin slices bacon (approximately 8 ounces), chilled in the freezer for 30 minutes*
²/₃ *cup heavy (whipping) cream*
Fine sea salt, for garnish
Grilled country bread rubbed with garlic, for serving

❋ Cut twenty-four 5-inch rounds from waxed paper. Trim the truffles so that they can be cut into thin, even rounds. Mince the truffle trimmings. Rub the waxed-paper rounds with the garlic halves. With a brush, generously coat the garlic side of each paper round with some of the melted butter. Brush one side of each truffle slice with the butter and beginning in the center of the buttered side of the paper rounds, arrange the truffle slices, buttered side down, in a circular pattern, overlapping them slightly. When all the truffle slices are arranged, brush the entire surface with a generous coating of butter. Top the truffles with a second paper round, butter side down, and press down firmly. Repeat to make 7 more tart bases (reserve the remaining 8 paper rounds). Cover and refrigerate the tart bases for at least 1 hour to harden the butter. (These truffle rounds may be prepared 6 to 8 hours in advance.)

❋ Cut the onions in half, place them, cut side down, on a cutting board, and then cut into very thin, almost transparent slices. Combine the onions and goose fat in a large skillet or sauté pan over low heat. Sprinkle with salt and pepper and cook for 10 minutes, stirring constantly. The onions should not color. Set them aside.

❋ Remove the bacon from the freezer. Trim the fat and cut the meat into very tiny cubes. Bring a small saucepan of water to a boil. Place the bacon in a small fine-meshed sieve and submerge it in the boiling water for 10 seconds. Set aside to drain.

❋ Add the truffle trimmings to the skillet with the onions and warm over low heat for approximately 30 seconds. Add the bacon, sprinkle generously with pepper, and stir constantly for 1 minute. Add the cream and cook for 1 minute more, stirring constantly. Taste for seasoning. The mixture should be quite peppery.

Antoine Vollon, *Mound of Butter* (1875/1885)

❀ Divide the onion mixture among 8 dinner plates. Flatten each mound to form a circle the size of the truffle rounds, placing the third paper round on top of each mound to use as a guide. Remove the paper.

❀ Preheat the oven to 475 degrees F. To assemble the tarts, remove the truffle rounds from the refrigerator, remove the top piece of paper from each round and invert the round onto an onion circle, leaving the remaining piece of paper on each truffle round intact. Place the plates in the oven for 1 minute, or just long enough to melt the butter that is holding the truffles together. As soon as the butter melts, remove the plates from the oven and carefully pull away the top layer of paper. Sprinkle with pepper and the fine sea salt, and serve with the grilled bread.

TO MAKE ONION AND BACON RAMEKINS: Divide the onion and bacon mixture among eight $^1/_2$-cup ramekins and even it out with the back of a spoon. Cover with plastic wrap and reheat in a microwave for 1 minute on high, or in a steamer until warmed through, approximately 3 to 4 minutes. Unmold onto warmed salad plates and serve immediately.

BEEF TENDERLOIN ROASTED IN AN HERB-INFUSED SALT CRUST/RÔTI DE FILET DE BOEUF EN CROÛTE DE SEL AUX HERBES

Serves 8

Beef tenderloin—known in France as the filet de boeuf—is one of the finest, juiciest, and leanest cuts of meat. Here, the meat is cooked in a salt crust, a marvelous method. The meat is first seared over high heat to seal in the juices, then roasted in the salt crust at a moderate temperature to ensure meat that is rare, juicy, and perfectly and evenly pink. As the roasted meat rests in the salt crust, it continues to cook, and the herbs and salt are drawn into the meat. Since beef tenderloin is naturally tender, it does not need a long cooking time.

When roasted in this manner, the beef cooks evenly, slices easily, and shrinks less, and there is no waste. It is a great dish for entertaining, for all the work is done ahead of time and the crust can be made 24 hours in advance. The roast needs no sauce, just a salad and a vegetable for accompaniment.

WINE SUGGESTION
A firm, elegant red Burgundy, such as Pommard

SALT CRUST
2 cups kosher salt*
1/4 cup fresh whole thyme leaves, or 2 tablespoons
    dried thyme
1 tablespoon minced fresh rosemary leaves, or
    1 1/2 teaspoons dried rosemary
2 large egg whites
2/3 cup water
3 cups all-purpose flour, or more if needed

BEEF
1 boneless beef tenderloin (approximately
    2 pounds) at room temperature
1 tablespoon unsalted butter
1 tablespoon extra virgin olive oil
1 large egg yolk
1 teaspoon water
1 teaspoon fresh whole thyme leaves, or
    1/2 teaspoon dried thyme
2 tablespoons coarse sea salt
Freshly ground black pepper to taste

❀ At least 3 1/2 hours before serving, prepare the salt crust: In the bowl of a heavy-duty electric mixer fitted with a paddle, combine the salt and herbs and mix to blend. Add the egg whites and water and mix until thoroughly blended. Add the flour, a little at a time, and knead until the mixture forms a firm, smooth dough, 2 to 3 minutes. The dough should be firm and not too moist or sticky, or the beef will steam, not roast. If necessary, knead in additional flour to make a firm dough. (The dough can also be mixed and kneaded carefully by hand in a large bowl.) Cover the dough with plastic wrap and let it rest at room temperature for a minimum of 2 hours, or for up to 24 hours. (This resting period will make the dough less sticky and easier to roll out.)

❀ Preheat the oven to 375 degrees F. To prepare the beef, pat the meat dry with paper towels. (Do not salt the meat at this point, or the flavorful juices will be drawn from the meat and will prevent it from browning evenly.) Heat the butter and oil in a large skillet or sauté pan over medium-high heat. Add the beef and sear well on all sides, 2 to 3 minutes per side. Place a salad plate upside down on a large platter. Transfer the seared beef to rest on the platter at an angle, propped on the salad plate. This will allow air to circulate evenly around the beef as it continues to cook while resting, which will help the meat to cook evenly and to remain tender. Let it rest for 5 minutes.

❀ Meanwhile, on a lightly floured board, roll the salt crust dough into a 15-by-10-inch rectangle, or one large enough to enclose the beef easily without stretching the dough. In a small bowl, mix the egg yolk and water together to make a glaze. Set aside.

❋ Just before roasting, sprinkle the beef with the thyme. (Do not wrap the beef in advance, or the meat and the salt crust will turn soggy.) Completely wrap the beef in the salt crust dough, pressing all the seams together to seal them well. Transfer the wrapped beef to a baking sheet. With a brush, coat the entire surface of the dough with the glaze. Sprinkle with the sea salt.

❋ Place the baking sheet in the middle shelf of the oven and roast the meat for 12 minutes per pound for rare (or until the interior registers 125 degrees F on a meat thermometer). For medium rare, roast an additional 3 to 4 minutes per pound. The crust should be a golden brown. Let the beef, which will continue to cook, rest in the crust on the baking sheet at room temperature for 1 hour (*see note below*). The beef will remain warm.

❋ To serve, slice off the crust at one end, remove the beef, and discard the crust. Season the beef with pepper, cut it on the diagonal into thick slices, and arrange on a warmed serving platter. Serve immediately.

Note: All meat—particularly this beef tenderloin roasted in a salt crust—should rest once it is removed from the oven. The resting time allows the juices to be reabsorbed into the meat, making the meat tender and easier to cut. (If you cut slices right away, all the flavorful juices will flow out, leaving tougher, less flavorful meat.)

*In general we prefer unrefined sea salt for cooking, preferably *sel de Guérande* from Brittany. But here the salt is simply used as a cooking vessel and will not be consumed, so kosher salt, which is far less expensive, is suggested.

Paul Gauguin, *Breton Girls Dancing, Pont-Aven* (1888)

Paul Gauguin,
Haystacks in Brittany (1890)

Edouard Vuillard, *Repast in a Garden* (1898)

FIELD SALAD WITH FRESH HERBS/
SALADE VERTE AUX HERBES FRAÎCHES

Serves 8

VINAIGRETTE
2 teaspoons best-quality red wine vinegar
2 teaspoons best-quality sherry wine vinegar
Sea salt to taste
1/4 cup extra virgin olive oil
Freshly ground white pepper to taste

1 cup loosely packed mixed fresh herb leaves, such as chervil, sage, tarragon, dill, basil, marjoram, flat-leaf parsley, and mint
4 cups loosely packed bite-sized pieces mixed salad greens, such as red- and green-tipped oakleaf lettuce, white- and green-tipped curly endive, radicchio, watercress, lamb's lettuce, dandelion greens, and arugula

❀ To prepare the vinaigrette, in a small bowl whisk together the vinegar and salt. Add the oil in a thin stream while whisking constantly until well blended. Season with pepper. Set aside.

❀ Carefully wash and spin dry the herb leaves and salad greens. In a large, shallow bowl, combine the herbs and salad greens, and toss with your hands. Pour the vinaigrette over the salad a little at a time and toss, gently and thoroughly, until all the herbs and greens are evenly coated. They should not "swim" in dressing. Serve immediately.

Joël Robuchon likes to say, "I made my reputation on salad and mashed potatoes." But what salad, and what mashed potatoes. It is indicative of his personality—he can only be "the best"—to try to woo diners with a perfect salad. He uses only the very tips of the freshest, most tender salad greens. (The "insides" of the leaves, the less tender portions, are set aside for the staff lunch.) He adds them to the leaves of a medley of the freshest of herbs. The choice, of course, is unlimited. The point is to come up with a salad of varied colors, textures, and pungencies.

Edouard Manet, *Two Apples* (c. 1880)

GOLDEN SUNBURST APPLE GALETTE
WITH CINNAMON ICE CREAM/
GALETTE FINE AUX POMMES ET GLACE À LA CANELLE

Makes one 10 ¹/₂-inch tart; serves 8

APPLE COMPOTE

2 *plump, moist vanilla beans*

2 *baking apples, such as Jonagold, Gala,
    Gravenstein, or Cortland*

3 *tablespoons water*

3 *tablespoons granulated sugar*

1 *tablespoon unsalted butter*

One 10 ¹/₂-inch partially baked rimless puff pastry
    shell (recipe follows), or 4 ounces store-bought
    puff pastry

3 *similar-sized baking apples, such as Jonagold,
    Gala, Gravenstein, or Cortland*

2 *tablespoons unsalted butter, melted*

2 *tablespoons granulated sugar*

Sifted confectioners' sugar for dusting

Cinnamon Ice Cream (recipe follows on p. 95)

*This delicious golden apple tart is
a cinch to prepare, and the layers
of apple—patterned like a
sunburst or the petals of a daisy—
make a very elegant presentation.
You do not have to tell people how
easy it is. The thin layer of
compote adds a smooth and
vibrant touch, a contrast to the
crispness of the apples.*

WINE SUGGESTION
A young Sauternes

❋ To prepare the apple compote, flatten the vanilla beans, cut them in half lengthwise, and scrape out the seeds with a small spoon. Place the seeds in a small bowl and set aside. Peel and core the apples and cut them into small cubes. Combine the apple cubes, water, sugar, and vanilla seeds in a medium saucepan and place over medium heat. Cover and cook until the apples are very soft, approximately 10 minutes; watch carefully and stir occasionally so they do not scorch. Remove from the heat, add the butter and stir to blend. Transfer the apples to a blender or a food processor fitted with the metal blade and purée until smooth; set aside to cool. (You should have approximately ²/₃ cup of compote.)

❋ Preheat the oven to 425 degrees F. To prepare the tart, spoon the cooled apple compote onto the cooled pastry and even it out with a thin, flexible spatula. Peel and carefully core the 3 apples with an apple corer, leaving the apples whole. Using a mandoline, electric slicer, or a sharp knife, cut the apples into very thin horizontal slices. With a round cookie cutter or top of a small juice glass, cut out a 2-inch circle from the side of an apple slice to use for decorating the center of the tart.

❋ Begin making a row of slices at the edge of the pastry shell, overlapping each slice to cover the hole in the center of the preceding slice and to cover the compote. When the first row is completed, brush it with melted butter. Continue with a second, inside row, slightly overlapping the apples from the outside row, as well as each apple slice in the inside row. Brush this row with melted butter. Place 2 or 3 overlapping slices in the center, again covering the hole in the center of each slice. Place the round slice of apple in the center and brush with melted butter. Sprinkle the entire tart evenly with granulated sugar.

❋ Place the tart on the middle shelf of the oven and bake until the apples are lightly golden, 20 to 25 minutes. Remove from the oven and, while still hot, sprinkle evenly and generously with confectioners' sugar. Preheat the broiler and place the tart under the broiler until golden brown, 1 to 2 minutes. Watch carefully so the sugar does not burn. Serve warm, with cinnamon ice cream.

PUFF PASTRY/PÂTE FEUILLETÉE

Makes 1 pound

TO PREPARE A PARTIALLY
BAKED RIMLESS PUFF PASTRY
SHELL: *Divide the puff pastry
into 4 equal parts, each approximately 4 ounces. Reserve 3
portions for another use. Butter the
bottom of a 10 1/2-inch tart pan
with a removable bottom and set
the pan aside. On a lightly floured
surface, carefully roll out the dough
into an 11-inch circle. Place the
removable tart bottom on the top of
the pastry, gently "marking" the
dough. (This will make it easier to
cut once the pastry is baked.)*

*Slip the tart bottom underneath
the pastry and place on a rimmed
baking sheet. Generously prick
the dough and refrigerate for
at least 30 minutes.*

*Preheat the oven to 450 degrees F.
Place the sheet on the top rack
of the oven, turn down the heat
immediately to 425 degrees F,
and bake the pastry for 10
minutes. Remove from the oven,
trim the edges so that they are
even, and then return to the oven
for 5 minutes without the baking
sheet. (Prebaking the shell can
be done several hours ahead.)*

5 *tablespoons unsalted butter, melted and cooled,
plus 10 tablespoons unsalted butter, chilled*
1/2 *teaspoon fine sea salt*

6 *tablespoons water*
1 1/2 *cups unbleached all-purpose flour, sifted,
plus more for dusting*

❀ Combine the melted butter, salt, and water in a small bowl and stir to blend. Place the flour in a food processor fitted with the metal blade. With the motor turning, slowly pour the melted butter mixture into the feed tube and process just until the dough begins to form a ball. The dough should be quite soft, but not sticky. (Do not work the dough too much or it will be elastic, and thus difficult to use.) Turn out onto a floured work surface. Press the dough together to form an even, flattened square. With a knife, lightly mark an X-shaped incision in the top of the dough, to make it easier to roll out when it is chilled. Wrap the dough in waxed paper and refrigerate for at least 30 minutes.

❀ Just before removing the dough from the refrigerator, place the chilled butter on top of a piece of waxed paper. With a rolling pin, slowly pound the butter to flatten it into a 4-inch square, pulling the paper up around the butter to help even the edges. Ideally, the pounded butter should have the same consistency as the dough.

❀ Lightly dust the work surface with flour, unwrap the dough, and place it on the work surface. With a knife, lightly re-mark the X-shaped incision in the center of the dough. With the heel of your hand, press out the 4 corners from the center of the dough, leaving a slightly mounded square in the center that is just slightly larger than the 4-inch square of butter. Roll the rolling pin out over the 4 corners to thin them, leaving the center mound slightly thicker. Place the pounded butter on top of the center mound. (If necessary, adjust the butter to fit the dough by making the square of butter smaller rather than larger.) Fold the dough flaps, one over the other, to cover the butter (as if forming an envelope), making an even 5-inch square. With the rolling pin, press down on the edges to seal, making sure that the butter is securely enclosed. Seal thoroughly, especially at the corners, but do not deform the square. Dust lightly with flour.

❀ *To make the first double turn,* using a rolling pin roll the square into a 15-inch-by-5-inch rectangle. Apply even pressure as you roll to ensure that the edges remain straight and that the dough does not widen. With a brush, dust off the excess flour. Fold the dough into thirds by bringing the end closest to you two-thirds of the way to the other end, and fold the remaining third over that. This should form a 3-layered square that measures approximately 5 inches. Turn the square to the left, one-fourth of a full turn (90 degrees), so that the "open" end of the fold is on the right and the "closed" side is on the left, like a book. Roll out into a 15-by-5-inch rectangle and fold in thirds again. This is the first turn. Rotate the dough again with the "open" end on the right, and repeat the rolling and folding operation one more time. The first double turn is now complete. Gently make 2 indentations with your fingers in the center of the dough to mark the first double turn. Wrap the dough in waxed paper and refrigerate for at least 30 minutes.

❧ *To make the second double turn,* proceed as for the first turn: Unwrap the dough. On a lightly floured surface, place the "open" side of the dough to the right and evenly roll out to a 15-by-5-inch rectangle. Dust off any excess flour. Rotate the dough again with the "open" end to the right, and repeat the rolling and folding operation one more time. The second double turn is now complete. Gently make 4 indentations with your fingers in the center of the dough to mark the second turn, wrap the dough in waxed paper, and refrigerate for 30 minutes. (The dough may be prepared up to 1 day in advance. If so, cover securely and refrigerate. It may also be frozen, securely wrapped, for several weeks. Defrost thoroughly—overnight, in the refrigerator—before continuing with the third double turn.)

❧ *To make the third double turn,* repeat the procedure for the second turn exactly. Wrap the dough in waxed paper and refrigerate for at least 30 minutes. The puff pastry is now ready to be rolled out and baked as desired.

Puff pastry is, essentially, alternating thin layers of butter and dough. The process of folding and rolling out superimposes these two elements. In the oven, the heat melts the butter, which then "fries," and it is this frying that lifts and separates the layers of dough. The pockets that form between the layers are created by the evaporation of the moisture in the dough and the butter. Puff pastry can be made in advance and frozen for up to 1 month.

CINNAMON ICE CREAM/GLACE À LA CANELLE

Makes 1 quart

1 ²/₃ cups whole milk
1 tablespoon freshly ground cinnamon
5 large egg yolks

²/₃ cup granulated sugar
³/₄ cup heavy (whipping) cream

❧ Combine the milk and cinnamon in a large saucepan and bring just to a boil. Remove from heat, cover, and set aside to infuse for 15 minutes. In a bowl, combine the egg yolks and sugar and beat with an electric mixer until thick and lemon colored. Set aside.

❧ Return the milk mixture to high heat and return to a boil. Pour one-third of the boiling milk into the egg yolk mixture, whisking constantly. Then whisk the milk-yolk mixture into the milk in the saucepan. Reduce the heat to low and cook, stirring constantly with a wooden spoon, until the mixture thickens to a creamy consistency. Do not let it boil. To test, run your finger down the back of the spoon: If the mixture is sufficiently cooked, the mark will hold. The whole process should take approximately 5 minutes.

❧ Remove the custard from the heat and immediately stir in the cream to stop the cooking. Pass the custard through a fine-meshed sieve. Let cool completely. (To speed the cooling, transfer the cream to a chilled large bowl. Place that bowl inside a slightly larger bowl filled with ice cubes and water. Stir occasionally. To test the temperature, dip your fingers into the mixture. The cream should feel cold to the touch. The process should take approximately 30 minutes.)

❧ When thoroughly cooled, transfer the custard to an ice cream maker and freeze according to the manufacturer's instructions.

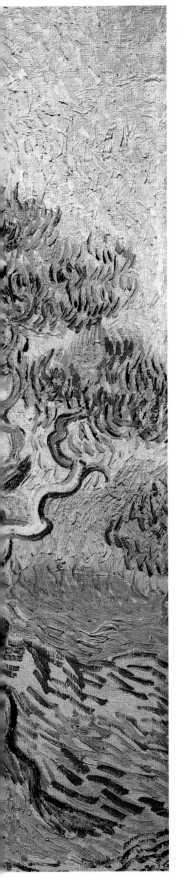

THE OLIVE ORCHARD
ALICE WATERS

*This olive orchard transports me straight to
Provence and its luscious, fragrant oil. I dream
of the bouillabaisse my friend Lulu cooks in a
huge copper cauldron over the olive wood and
vine branches from her vineyard. Every part
of an olive tree is beautiful and useful: the
gnarled trunks, the gray-green leaves, and
the black and green fruits.*

A DINNER MENU

Roasted Almonds

Mesclun Salad with
Tapenade Croutons

La Bouillabaisse Chez Panisse

Meyer Lemon Sherbet

Vincent van Gogh,
The Olive Orchard (1889)

Vincent van Gogh, *Farmhouse in Provence* (1888)

ROASTED ALMONDS

Serves 8

❋ Preheat the oven to 350 degrees F. Place 2 cups of organically grown, new-crop almonds, shelled, on a baking sheet. Roast the almonds in the oven for 10 minutes, or until they are quite browned and aromatic. Toss with a sprinkling of salt and let cool slightly before serving.

MESCLUN SALAD WITH TAPENADE CROUTONS

Serves 8

VINAIGRETTE
2 shallots, cut into very thin slices
A pinch of salt
¹/₄ cup red wine vinegar
¹/₂ cup extra virgin olive oil

8 large handfuls (approximately 1 pound) mesclun
(mixture of fresh chervil sprigs, young arugula,
dandelion greens, and young oakleaf lettuce)
Tapenade Croutons (recipe follows)

❋To make the vinaigrette, place the shallots in a small bowl with the salt and vinegar. Let the shallots soak in the vinegar for 15 to 20 minutes, then stir in the olive oil and mix well. Taste to see if the balance of the vinegar and oil is right—you might need to add more of one or the other.

❋Wash the greens gently in a large bowl of cold water. Drain and spin them dry in a salad spinner or lettuce dryer, filling it only half full at a time. It is important to have dry lettuces, so the dressing will coat the leaves. As the greens are dried, spread them out on a towel. Roll the towel up loosely and refrigerate the greens until you are ready to serve them.

❋Place the greens in a large bowl. Drizzle on the vinaigrette a little at a time and toss the greens; add only enough dressing to just coat the leaves. Taste for seasoning and serve with the tapenade croutons.

TAPENADE CROUTONS

Serves 8

4 dozen Gaeta olives (approximately 2 cups),
*   pitted*
¹/₃ cup olive oil
1 ¹/₂ salt-packed anchovies, rinsed and filleted

1 or 2 garlic cloves
A dash of Cognac
16 baguette slices, each approximately
*   ¹/₄-inch thick*

Because the intense flavors of the ingredients are so variable, the tapenade must be made by taste and not by amount. The idea is to balance the flavors so that no one element dominates the others. A dash of Cognac provides a sweetness and harmony to the sauce.

❋Purée the olives with the olive oil in a blender or, alternatively, chop them finely by hand and mix in the oil. Pound the anchovies to a smooth paste in a mortar. Pound the garlic to a paste in another mortar. Blend a little of the anchovies and a little of the garlic with the olives, adding each by degrees, and tasting as you go. Add a dash of Cognac to taste. Let the tapenade sit for an hour or so for the flavors to marry.

❋Preheat the oven to 400 degrees F. Place the bread slices on a baking sheet and toast them in the oven for approximately 5 minutes, or until they are lightly browned. While the croutons are still warm, spread them with the tapenade.

Auguste Renoir, *Girl with a Basket of Fish* (c. 1889)   Auguste Renoir, *Girl with a Basket of Oranges* (c. 1889)

LA BOUILLABAISSE CHEZ PANISSE

Serves 8 to 10

One very fresh whole rockfish (rock cod, snapper,
    sea bass, halibut), approximately 8 pounds
1 whole ocean perch or anglerfish, approximately
    2 pounds

MARINADE
Approximately 1/2 cup virgin olive oil
Approximately 2 cups dry white wine
2 fresh thyme sprigs
2 sprigs fresh fennel tops
6 fresh parsley sprigs
3 garlic cloves
2 tablespoons Pernod
A pinch of saffron

FUMET
Reserved fish bones, heads, and trimmings
2 carrots
1 leek
1 yellow onion
2 vine-ripened tomatoes
6 cultivated field or white mushrooms
1/3 cup olive oil
2 garlic cloves, unpeeled
Bouquet garni: 6 parsley sprigs, 1 teaspoon fennel
    seeds, 2 bay leaves, 1/2 teaspoon dried
    tarragon, 1/2 teaspoon dried thyme, 10 to 12
    black peppercorns, and 6 to 8 coriander seeds
2 cups dry white wine
6 mussels in the shells, debearded and well-scrubbed
6 clams, well-scrubbed
Zest of 1 small orange, with no white pith
2 tablespoons Pernod
A pinch of saffron
A pinch of cayenne pepper

ROUILLE
1 vine-ripened tomato
1 red bell pepper

1/4 cup strained fumet
A pinch each of saffron and cayenne pepper
1 slice good white bread, crust removed
5 to 8 garlic cloves
3 egg yolks
3/4 cup virgin olive oil
3/4 cup mild olive oil
Salt, freshly ground black pepper, saffron, and
    cayenne pepper to taste

GARLIC CROUTONS
24 baguette slices, each approximately 3/8 inch thick
Approximately 1/2 cup virgin olive oil
2 to 3 garlic cloves, halved

BROTH
1/4 cup virgin olive oil
2 leeks, white part only, carefully washed and cut
    into 1/2-inch dice
2 onions, cut into 1/2-inch dice
1 bay leaf
A pinch of saffron
Salt and freshly ground black pepper to taste
Remaining warm strained fumet
3 garlic cloves, minced
1 fresh fennel sprig
1 fresh parsley sprig
Zest of 1/2 small orange, with no white pith
4 very ripe large tomatoes, peeled, seeded, and diced
1 cup dry white wine
Pernod to taste
1 1/2 dozen mussels in the shells, debearded and
    well-scrubbed
3 1/2 dozen clams, well-scrubbed
Marinated fish

1/4 cup minced fresh parsley, for garnish
10 to 12 fresh basil leaves, for garnish

Many ingredients are needed to
make a wonderful bouillabaisse;
however, the ingredients are easy to
obtain and some of the preparation
may be done in advance. There are
two important things to remember
when making a bouillabaisse:
The fish and shellfish must be
absolutely fresh, and the saffron
and Pernod must be added with
a light hand. The rouille in
this recipe is a spicy Provençal,
mayonnaise-like sauce.

WINE SUGGESTION
A Bandol rosé, such as
Domaine Tempier, or a chilled
young Bandol rouge

❈ Fillet both fish, reserving the heads, bones, and scraps for the *fumet*. Cut the fillets into even pieces 2 inches long and 1 inch thick. The thickness should be equal for all pieces; the length can vary.

❈ To make the marinade, combine the marinade ingredients in a large nonaluminum bowl. Add the fish, cover, and marinate at room temperature for 2 hours, or cover and refrigerate for several hours.

❈ To make the fumet, wash the fish scraps under cold running water, making sure to remove any bloody parts; cut out and discard the gills. Chop the carrots, leek, onion, tomatoes, and mushrooms coarsely. Heat the oil in a heavy, 12-quart stockpot over medium heat. Add the vegetables, garlic, and fish scraps and cook gently for 10 to 12 minutes. Place the bouquet garni ingredients in cheesecloth and tie it closed with cotton string. Add the bouquet garni to the stockpot, along with the wine and cold water to cover. Add the remaining fumet ingredients and bring to a boil. Reduce the heat immediately, and simmer, skimming frequently, for approximately 30 minutes. Let the fumet stand off the heat for 15 minutes, then strain it. If the fumet is being made in advance, let it cool to room temperature, then cover and refrigerate it until needed. Simply warm it before adding it to the broth.

❈ To make the *rouille,* roast the tomato and bell pepper on a grill, over an open flame, or under a preheated broiler, turning to blacken all sides. When the tomato is browned and softened, remove it from the heat using a metal spatula and let cool. When the skin of the pepper is black, place the pepper in a plastic or paper bag, close it, and let sit until the pepper is cool enough to handle, approximately 5 minutes. Peel the skin from the pepper and discard the seeds and stem. Cut the tomato in half crosswise and spoon out the seeds. Place the $1/4$ cup fumet in a medium bowl, mix in the saffron and cayenne, and soak the slice of bread in the fumet for several minutes until it is very soft. Crush the garlic to a paste in a mortar. Using a whisk, beat the egg yolks and garlic into the bread. Mix the olive oil together and begin whisking into the egg mixture, a few drops at a time, until it emulsifies. Continue to whisk in the oil in a fine stream until a thick mayonnaise is formed. Make a purée of the roasted pepper and tomato in a large mortar and stir it into the mayonnaise. Season with salt, pepper, saffron, and cayenne. Cover and refrigerate until needed.

❈ To make the croutons, preheat the oven to 400 degrees F. Lightly brush the baguette slices with the oil and bake for 5 minutes, or until golden brown. Rub the croutons with the cut garlic cloves while they are still warm. Set aside.

❈ To make the broth, heat the oil in a large, heavy pan over medium heat. Add the leeks, onions, bay leaf, saffron, and salt and pepper and sauté for 10 minutes, or until the leeks and onions are tender. Add the remaining fumet, garlic, fennel, parsley, zest, tomatoes, wine, and Pernod. Add the clams and mussels, cover, and steam for 1 to 2 minutes, or until they begin to open. Remove the fish from the marinade with a slotted spoon, lifting out the larger pieces first, add to the broth, and cook for 3 minutes, or until the fish are opaque and all the shellfish have opened. Do not stir, or the fish will break. Using the slotted spoon, remove the fish and shellfish to large individual serving bowls. Bring the broth to a boil and season with whatever is necessary—oil, wine, Pernod, saffron, cayenne, or salt.

❈ To serve, ladle the broth over the fish. Tuck 3 croutons in at the sides of each bowl, spoon the rouille over the fish, and garnish with the parsley and basil.

Maurice de Vlaminck, *Still Life with Lemons,* detail (1913/1914)

MEYER LEMON SHERBET

Makes approximately 1 quart

3 *good-sized Meyer lemons*
1 *cup plus 3 tablespoons granulated sugar*
4 *cups water*
Regular lemon juice to taste (optional)

2 *tablespoons champagne or dry white wine*
  (optional)
8 *fresh mint sprigs, for garnish*

Meyer lemons are sweeter and more aromatic than regular lemons. Meyer lemon trees can produce all year round, but the biggest crops are in late fall through spring. If you must substitute the more acidic juice of regular lemons, mix in a little fresh orange juice or increase the amount of sugar to taste.

❈ Wash the lemons and shred the zest of 1 lemon into a medium nonaluminum bowl. Try to produce long $1/16$-inch-wide shreds of the zest, being careful not to cut into the bitter white pith under the zest. Juice all of the lemons, measure $3/4$ cup of the juice, and strain it through a sieve into the bowl with the zest, pushing as much of the pulp through the sieve as you can.

❈ Combine the sugar and 1 cup of the water in a medium saucepan and heat, stirring, until the sugar is completely dissolved. Stir in the remaining 3 cups of cold water and then stir this into the juice and zest. Taste and add a little more juice if needed. Late in their season, Meyer lemons may be quite sweet and need some regular lemon juice added for tartness.

❈ Add the wine at this point, if desired. (The wine will make a creamier sherbet because alcohol does not freeze.) Cover and refrigerate the mixture until well chilled, then freeze it in an ice cream maker according to the manufacturer's instructions. Serve in chilled dishes, garnished with sprigs of mint.

STILL LIFE WITH APPLES
ON A PINK TABLECLOTH
PAULA WOLFERT

This marvelous painting by Matisse calls gently to me. Looking at it, I feel the easy warmth of an autumnal sun and see dazzling Mediterranean light. I also see in Matisse's painted canvas a canvas I myself can fill. You see, for me an empty space on a table is an invitation to cook and nurture. The meal, of course, must be French. As for those apples— I know just what to do with them!

A DINNER MENU

Smoked Salmon with Mixed Melon

Roasted Leg of Lamb with Tarragon,
Anchovies, and Cornichons

Mashed Potatoes with Olive Oil

Salade de Canaille with
Sour Grape Juice

Apples Baked on Cabbage Leaves
as in Poitou

Henri Matisse, *Still Life with
Apples on a Pink Tablecloth* (1924)

SMOKED SALMON WITH MIXED MELON

Serves 4 to 6

This delicate, refined appetizer is similar in concept to the classic melon with prosciutto, exploiting an unexpected affinity by matching the rich texture of salmon with the sweet, refreshing quality of melon and the acidity of grapefruit. For the richest fruit flavor, let the melon steep with the grapefruit for an hour or so before mixing it with the salmon.

WINE SUGGESTION
A crisp Voignier, such as Condrieu

6 ounces smoked salmon, preferably Scottish or
    Norwegian, thinly sliced
2 cups cut crenshaw, casaba, or Spanish melon
    ($^3/_4$-by-$^3/_4$-by-$^1/_4$-inch)
2 cups cut honeydew melon ($^3/_4$-by-$^3/_4$-by-
    $^1/_4$-inch)

2 cups cut cantaloupe ($^3/_4$-by-$^3/_4$-by-$^1/_4$-inch)
$^1/_3$ cup cubed grapefruit flesh
2 tablespoons fresh orange juice
3 tablespoons fresh lemon juice
2 tablespoons extra virgin olive oil
Salt and freshly ground black pepper to taste

❈ Cut the smoked salmon slices into $^3/_4$-inch squares, place in a bowl, cover, and refrigerate until well chilled. Combine the melon and grapefruit in a large nonaluminum bowl, cover, and refrigerate until well chilled.

❈ Just before serving, add the salmon to the fruit, along with the fresh juices and olive oil. Season lightly with salt and generously with pepper. Toss to mix. Serve in individual cups.

Edouard Manet, *Still Life with Melon and Peaches* (c. 1866)

ROASTED LEG OF LAMB WITH TARRAGON, ANCHOVIES, AND CORNICHONS

Serves 4 to 6

My recipe for this flavorful and aromatic dish was inspired by an old French preparation, gigot de mouton à la genoise, which appears in Menon's eighteenth-century cookbook, La cuisine bourgeoisie. The leg is stuffed, then wrapped in caul fat, which makes it partially self-basting. For a wonderful crisp crust, the lamb is basted additionally by hand. Remember: If you do not baste, you will be baking the lamb, rather than roasting it.

WINE SUGGESTION
A red Bordeaux

Approximately 5 ounces caul fat*
1 leg of spring lamb, or shortened leg (shank half), leg bone intact (approximately 4 pounds)
1 teaspoon freshly ground black pepper
1 1/2 teaspoons minced garlic
4 1/2 tablespoons olive oil
2 celery stalks, minced (approximately 3/4 cup)
1 onion, minced (approximately 3/4 cup)
3 ounces prosciutto or Westphalian ham, minced

One 2-ounce can flat anchovy fillets, oil-packed, drained, rinsed, soaked in milk for 10 minutes, rinsed, and mashed to a purée
2 teaspoons minced fresh tarragon
2 tablespoons finely chopped cornichons (approximately 5)
1 teaspoon plus 1/3 cup white wine vinegar
1/2 teaspoon salt
2 shallots, minced
1/3 cup dry white wine
3/4 cup unsalted lamb or chicken stock

❀ Soak the caul fat in several changes of vinegared water to cover for approximately 30 minutes. Ask the butcher to partially bone the lamb for you, or do it yourself by working a thin-bladed knife around the hip end of the leg bone. Loosen the meat around the bone until you reach the joint, then twist the bone to remove it. Do not remove the shank bone.

❀ Season the inside of the lamb with 1/2 teaspoon of the pepper and 1/2 teaspoon of the garlic. Heat half of the olive oil in a medium skillet or sauté pan over medium heat. Add the celery and onion and cook, stirring occasionally, until softened but not browned, approximately 10 minutes. Add the prosciutto and cook for 2 minutes. Remove the pan from the heat. Stir in the anchovies, the remaining 1 teaspoon garlic, the tarragon, cornichons, and the 1 teaspoon vinegar. Set aside to cool.

❀ Approximately 1 1/2 hours before serving, preheat the oven to 475 degrees F. Stuff the leg of lamb with the anchovy mixture and press the opening shut. Drain the caul fat and spread it out on a work surface. Place the stuffed leg of lamb, rounded side up, in the center and wrap it completely in the caul fat. Brush the lamb with the remaining half of the olive oil and sprinkle it with the salt and the remaining 1/2 teaspoon pepper. Place the lamb in a roasting pan and roast in the oven, uncovered, for 15 minutes.

❀ Meanwhile, in a small nonaluminum saucepan, combine the shallots, white wine, and the 1/3 cup vinegar. Bring to a boil over high heat, reduce the heat, and simmer until the liquid is reduced to 1/3 cup, approximately 10 minutes. Drain the shallots, reserving both the shallots and liquid.

Edward Hicks, *The Cornell Farm* (1848)

❀ Reduce the oven temperature to 350 degrees F and continue roasting the lamb, basting it often with the pan juices, for approximately 30 to 35 minutes, or until the internal temperature reaches 125 degrees F. Remove the meat to a warmed platter. Cover the lamb loosely with aluminum foil and let it rest in a warm place for 20 minutes. The lamb will continue to cook as it rests. For medium-rare lamb, the internal temperature should be 135 to 140 degrees F.

❀ Spoon off the fat from the pan juices. Pour the vinegar-wine liquid into the pan, then add the reserved shallots and stock; bring the mixture to a boil over high heat, stirring to scrape up the browned bits from the bottom of the pan, then reduce heat and simmer for 5 minutes to blend the flavors. Adjust the seasoning. Slice the lamb and arrange the slices overlapping on a warmed platter. Serve the shallot sauce on the side.

*Caul fat, a lacy, fatty membrane that melts as it cooks, must be ordered from a butcher shop. It is well worth looking for. When you order caul fat, buy several pounds, then freeze it in 8-ounce packets. (It can be kept up to 1 year in the freezer.) Use it for cooking lamb, sausages, salmon, and pork terrines. To prepare caul fat, soak it for approximately 30 minutes in several changes of vinegared water (1 teaspoon vinegar per 1 cup water).

Jean Siméon Chardin, *The Kitchen Maid* (1738)

MASHED POTATOES WITH OLIVE OIL

Serves 4 to 6

2 pounds Idaho potatoes
2 tablespoons coarse sea salt
$^1/_3$ cup mild extra virgin olive oil
$^3/_4$ to 1 cup whole milk, heated

Freshly ground white pepper to taste
A pinch of salt
A pinch of freshly grated nutmeg
2 tablespoons unsalted butter at room temperature

❋ Peel the potatoes and carefully remove any discolored parts. Leave them whole (or they will be watery). Place them in a 4-quart pot and add water to cover. Add the sea salt. Cover the pot and bring it to a boil. Reduce the heat to *just below* the boil and cook the potatoes for 45 minutes, or until they are tender when pierced with a thin skewer.

❋ Drain the potatoes well, return them to the saucepan, and cover with a towel and a lid. Let them stand until dry, approximately 5 minutes. Cut the potatoes into small pieces and press them through a ricer or the fine-holed disk of a food mill placed over the saucepan. Beat them vigorously with a wooden spoon until light and fluffy, while adding the olive oil by spoonfuls; then gradually beat in the heated milk. (The slower and longer you beat them, the more milk the potatoes will absorb, and the lighter and fluffier they will be.) Cover them with a piece of plastic wrap to prevent crusting. The potatoes may be kept hot in a double boiler for up to 2 hours.

❋ Just before serving, combine the pepper, salt, and nutmeg with the softened butter and beat it into the potatoes. Serve the potatoes very hot.

Mashed potatoes can be watery, lumpy, and tasteless, the way they are in school dining halls—or they can be celestial. One famous French recipe calls for as much as 2 cups of butter for every 2 pounds of potatoes! I certainly like to eat celestial mashed potatoes, but prefer not to consume so large a quantity of saturated fat. After experimenting a bit, I came up with the following recipe, which combines olive oil and milk with a last-minute addition of only 2 tablespoons of butter. The result is a convincing illusion of butter. You will not, in fact, taste the olive oil; it is there to add richness and to heighten the natural flavor of the potatoes.

Joseph Decker, *Grapes* (c. 1890/1895)

SALADE DE CANAILLE WITH SOUR GRAPE JUICE

Serves 4 to 6

1/2 teaspoon salt

1 1/2 tablespoons sour grape juice/verjus* (recipe
 follows) or a mild but fruity white wine
 vinegar, or more to taste

2 1/2 tablespoons extra virgin olive oil

1 tablespoon imported walnut oil

1/4 teaspoon freshly ground black pepper

4 to 5 cups mixed mild and bitter greens

1 teaspoon minced fresh chives

1 teaspoon minced fresh parsley

3 large basil leaves, rolled and cut into thin strips

1 teaspoon finely grated orange zest

3 small shallots, minced

According to my French dictionary, canaille *means "riffraff." I use this word to describe one of my favorite salads, a potpourri of ingredients that achieves a flavorful balance of textures, tastes, and smells. It is important to choose greens with a lot of character, so that each type holds its own: peppery arugula, bitter, curly white endive, and a few torn pieces of sharp radicchio, balanced by such sweet-tasting greens as lamb's lettuce (mâche) and Bibb.*

❧ In a mixing bowl, dissolve the salt in the *verjus* or vinegar; then beat in the oils. Season with pepper. Correct the acidity with more verjus or vinegar if necessary. Let the dressing sit while washing and drying the greens. Place the greens in a bowl and toss with the vinaigrette; then scatter the herbs, orange zest, and shallots on top. Serve at once on individual plates.

* Verjus, also called verjuice, may be purchased at specialty food stores, or you can make your own. Summer and fall are the times to make this delicious condiment, a specially made sour grape juice. It has a subtly sharp, thoroughly refreshing taste that enhances the flavor of green salads, chicken, foie gras, wild birds, trout, and stewed wild mushrooms. It may also be used in sauces.

SOUR GRAPE JUICE/VERJUS

❧ To make verjus, choose the sourest green grapes available. Holding on to the thick stem, dip them by the bunch into boiling water for 3 seconds to kill the surface yeasts. Remove the grapes at once and drain on a towel. Roll the grapes in a towel to dry them, then remove the grapes from the stems. Discard any blemished grapes. When dry, place the grapes in a blender or a food processor fitted with the metal blade and purée for 10 seconds; then strain, pressing down on the fruit to extract all the juice. Let stand for 10 minutes, then ladle the juice into a sieve lined with damp cheesecloth and strain again. Use fresh verjus at once, or freeze in plastic ice cube trays. For maximum flavor, use immediately on defrosting. Frozen verjus will keep for 3 months.

APPLES BAKED ON CABBAGE LEAVES AS IN POITOU

Makes one 12-inch tart; serves 4 to 6

When I first heard about this French dish, called grimolles, *I recalled a famous nonsense line of the eighteenth-century satirical dramatist Samuel Foote: "So she went into the garden to cut a cabbage leaf to make an apple pie . . ." In this unusual, earthy dessert, the cabbage leaves, used in place of a pie crust, act as a conductor for even cooking. A skillet is first lined with the leaves, and a mixture of apples and thick batter, flavored with lemon zest, Cognac, and cinnamon, is baked on top. The slightly burnt cabbage, which can be eaten or not, as you wish, imparts a marvelous smoky flavor to the fruit. I assure you that this will be a memorable closing to a meal. Serve it warm for best results. Vanilla ice cream, unsweetened crème fraîche, or whipped cream is an excellent accompaniment.*

3/4 cup unbleached all-purpose flour

2 eggs

1/4 cup heavy (whipping) cream at room temperature

1/2 cup milk at room temperature

A pinch of salt

2 dashes of ground cinnamon

2 teaspoons grated lemon zest

1 tablespoon Cognac

3 to 4 tablespoons granulated sugar

4 tablespoons (1/2 stick) unsalted butter, melted

1 pound flavorful apples

Approximately 6 large cabbage leaves

1 tablespoon packed light brown sugar

Sifted confectioners' sugar

❋ At least 2 hours before serving (so the batter has time to sit), place the flour in a medium bowl. With a wooden spoon, make a well in the center and add the eggs, one at a time, stirring until well combined. Then slowly add the cream and milk and mix until absolutely smooth. If the mixture is not smooth, strain it through a fine-meshed sieve. Flavor it with salt, cinnamon, lemon zest, and Cognac. Sweeten it with sugar (the amount depends on the sweetness of the apples). Stir in half of the melted butter.

❋ Peel, core, and quarter the apples. Cut them into 1/8-inch-thick slices and fold the slices into the batter. Cover the batter and let it sit at room temperature for approximately 1 hour.

❋ One hour before serving, preheat the oven to 425 degrees F. Heat a dry, nonstick skillet over medium heat and wilt and soften the cabbage leaves one at a time. Spread the cabbage leaves out, rib side down, in a well-seasoned 12-inch cast-iron skillet or black pizza pan, or on a 12-inch round cast-iron griddle; flatten them to cover the pan without overlapping them more than is necessary. Spread the apple batter over the cabbage in a thin, even layer. Sprinkle the brown sugar and the remaining melted butter on top.

❋ Bake the tart on the middle shelf of the oven for approximately 40 minutes, or until it is golden brown. (The center should still be slightly supple.) Remove the tart from the oven, dust it with confectioners' sugar, and serve hot from the pan, or slide it onto a large serving plate along with the cabbage leaves.

Netherlandish, *Head of Cabbage with Insects* (early seventeenth century)

Giovanni Bellini and Titian, *The Feast of the Gods* (1514/1529)

THE FEAST OF THE GODS

LORENZA DE' MEDICI

I think of cooking as being like painting, for beauty, color, and form are very important in preparing food. Often when I look at a painting it evokes food, and that is especially so with The Feast of the Gods, *which I admire whenever I visit Washington. This menu should have the flavor of the Renaissance, and what could be better for that than wild boar? People ate mainly wild game then, such as pheasant, hare, venison, and boar, which was perfumed with spices rather than the herbs we now use. A Renaissance banquet was a festive occasion of abundance and richness, and princes and popes commissioned the finest artists and artisans to create beautiful settings for their tables. The food itself was sculptural. One of the most famed presentations was a triumph of puff pastry containing live birds, which, when the pastry was cut, flew out and around the room.*

This feast begins in traditional style with a grand tuna mousse surrounded by golden, translucent gelatin that sparkles under candlelight. The menu continues with sweet-and-sour wild boar, enriched with prunes and choco-late, and concludes with light and crusty spiced cannoli filled with cream and candied fruit.

A DINNER MENU

Tuna Mousse/*Spuma di Tonno*

Wild Boar in Sweet-and-Sour
Chocolate Sauce/
Cinghiale in Dolceforte

Glazed Baby Onions with Raisins/
Cipolline all'Uvetta

Spiced Cannoli/*Cannoli alle Spezie*

TUNA MOUSSE/SPUMA DI TONNO

Serves 6

WINE SUGGESTION

*A dry white wine, such as
Trappoline (Coltibuono)*

2 *cups beef broth, warmed*
2 *tablespoons (2 packages) unflavored gelatin*
1 *whole egg*
2 *egg yolks*
1 ¼ *cups extra virgin olive oil*
A pinch of salt

Juice of 1 lemon
4 *large boiling potatoes*
1 *pound tuna in water*
3 *tablespoons capers, drained*
4 *oil-packed anchovy fillets, drained*

❀ Place the broth in a medium bowl and stir in the gelatin until it is dissolved. Pour the mixture onto a platter and refrigerate for at least 3 hours, or until set. Chop the gelatin finely and refrigerate again until needed.

❀ Place the whole egg and egg yolks in a blender or in a food processor fitted with the metal blade and blend until thick and foamy. With the motor running, add the oil in a very fine stream until a mayonnaise forms. Blend in the salt and lemon juice and transfer to a bowl. Cover and refrigerate until needed.

❀ Place the potatoes in a large saucepan of salted water and bring to a boil. Cook for approximately 40 minutes, or until tender; drain. While the potatoes are still hot, peel them and pass them through a food mill or ricer placed over a medium bowl. Pass the tuna, 2 tablespoons of the capers, and the anchovies through the food mill into the same bowl; or transfer them to a blender or a food processor fitted with the metal blade and purée until smooth, and add to the bowl. Stir together the potatoes and tuna mixture until well blended, then pour it into an oiled 6-cup ring mold, pressing the mixture down to pack the mold well. Smooth the surface before unmolding it onto a large serving platter.

❀ Cover the tuna completely with the mayonnaise and smooth the surface with the blade of a knife dipped in cold water. Cover and refrigerate the mousse for several hours. To serve, surround the mousse with the chopped gelatin and sprinkle the mousse with the remaining 1 tablespoon of capers.

Antonio Maria Vassallo, *The Larder* (probably c. 1650/1660)

Master of the Catholic Kings, *The Marriage at Cana* (c. 1495/1497)

WILD BOAR IN SWEET-AND-SOUR CHOCOLATE SAUCE/ CINGHIALE IN DOLCEFORTE

Serves 6

3 pounds boar, rump roast, or another suitable cut
    of beef for braising
2 carrots, roughly chopped
2 celery stalks, roughly chopped
2 yellow onions, roughly chopped
1/2 bottle aged Chianti Classico or other Italian
    dry red wine
1/4 cup extra virgin olive oil
1 tablespoon juniper berries
2 bay leaves

Salt to taste
1 teaspoon freshly ground black pepper
1/2 cup granulated sugar
4 garlic cloves, chopped coarsely
1 tablespoon water
1/2 cup red wine vinegar
2 ounces bitter chocolate, grated
1 cup pitted prunes, soaked in water until plumped
1/4 cup pine nuts

Although boar was commonly consumed during the Renaissance, you could easily substitute any kind of stew meat with rewarding results in this agrodolce dish.

❋ Twenty-four hours before cooking the meat, place it in a large glass casserole. Add the carrots, celery, and onions and mix well. Pour in the wine, cover, and refrigerate for 24 hours, turning the meat from time to time.

❋ The morning of serving, remove the meat from the marinade and pat it dry with paper towels. Strain the marinade and reserve both the marinade and the vegetables. Select a flameproof casserole with a lid or Dutch oven just large enough to hold the meat, pour the olive oil in it and place over high heat until it turns slightly brown. Add the meat and sear it on all sides, until well browned. Add the reserved vegetables, juniper berries, bay leaves, and salt and pepper to the meat and then pour the reserved marinade over the meat. Cover and simmer the meat over low heat for approximately 3 hours, or until tender. Turn off the heat and let the meat cool in the liquid. Spoon off as much fat from the surface of the liquid as possible.

❋ Approximately one hour before serving, remove the meat from the pot. Strain the cooking liquid, reserving the vegetables and the liquid. Return the liquid to the pot. Pass the vegetables through a food mill and mix them into the liquid in the pot. Return the meat to the pot, cover, and cook it over low heat for approximately 20 minutes.

❋ Meanwhile, combine the sugar, garlic, and water in a small saucepan over medium heat and cook until the sugar turns a light amber. Add the vinegar and chocolate and boil for approximately 3 minutes, or until the chocolate melts.

❋ Pour the warm chocolate mixture over the meat. Add the prunes, and pine nuts and simmer together for 10 minutes. Transfer the meat to a platter, pour the sauce over the top, and serve.

Pensionante del Saraceni, *Still Life with Fruit and Carafe* (c. 1610/1620)

GLAZED BABY ONIONS WITH RAISINS/
CIPOLLINE ALL'UVETTA

Serves 6

Cipolline onions are delicate, exceptionally sweet, white-fleshed onions traditionally used in Italian cuisine. They are slightly flattened spheres, typically larger than most pearl onions, and can be found in specialty markets in the United States.

WINE SUGGESTION
An aged Chianti Classico

2 *pounds cipolline onions or any variety of pearl onions*
1 *tablespoon unsalted butter*
1 *tablespoon extra virgin olive oil*
¹/₄ *cup water*

Salt and freshly ground black pepper to taste
¹/₃ *cup red wine vinegar*
6 *tablespoons granulated sugar*
¹/₂ *cup dark raisins*

❀ Peel the dry skin from the onions with a paring knife. Place the onions in a medium saucepan with the butter, oil, water, salt and pepper. Bring to a boil and then simmer for 30 minutes, or until tender. Remove from the heat and set aside.

❀ Place the vinegar in a small nonaluminum pan, stir in the sugar, and place over high heat and boil for 5 minutes. Pour the hot vinegar mixture over the onions and add the raisins. Place over low heat and cook for approximately 5 minutes, or until the sauce has reduced to a glaze. Serve immediately.

SPICED CANNOLI/CANNOLI ALLE SPEZIE

Serves 6

CANNOLI

2 *cups unbleached all-purpose flour*

$1/4$ *cup granulated sugar*

4 *tablespoons cold unsalted butter, cut into*
   small pieces

$1/4$ *cup dry Marsala*

1 *egg, beaten*

6 *cups vegetable oil for deep-frying*

FILLING

2 *cups ricotta cheese*

1 *tablespoon unsweetened cocoa powder*

1 *teaspoon ground cinnamon*

1 *teaspoon ground cloves*

$3/4$ *cup granulated sugar*

$1/4$ *cup candied orange peel, diced*

$1/4$ *cup candied citron peel, diced*

GARNISH

12 *candied cherries*

$1/2$ *cup confectioners' sugar, sifted*

For this recipe you will need twelve cannoli cylinders. They can be found in kitchenware stores.

BEVERAGE SUGGESTIONS
Vin Santo
Grappa
Caffè espresso

❧ To make the cannoli, mix the flour and sugar together in a bowl. Add the butter and cut in with a pastry cutter or your fingers until the mixture is crumbly. Stir in the Marsala and enough water to form a dough. Turn the dough out on a lightly floured board and knead it for approximately 10 minutes, or until smooth. Cover the dough with plastic wrap and refrigerate for approximately 2 hours.

❧ On a lightly floured surface roll out the dough into a $1/8$-inch-thick sheet. Cut out twelve 4- to 5-inch rounds with a pastry cutter and wrap each one around a cannoli tube. Seal the edges where they join by brushing the bottom edge with the beaten egg.

❧ Place the oil in a large, heavy pot or deep fryer and heat to 350 degrees F, or until almost smoking. Add the cannoli, a few at a time, and deep-fry for approximately 3 minutes, or until golden. Remove the cannoli with tongs and drain them on paper towels. Let cool completely on paper towels and carefully slide the tubes out.

❧ To make the filling, combine the ricotta, cocoa, cinnamon, cloves, and granulated sugar in a medium bowl and stir to mix well. Stir in the candied orange and citron peel. Place the filling in a pastry bag fitted with a large plain tube and pipe the filling into the cannoli. Press a cherry lightly into the ricotta at each end of the cannoli. Dust the cannoli with the confectioners' sugar and serve within approximately 30 minutes.

Wayne Thiebaud, *Cakes* (1963)

CAKES

NANCY SILVERTON

Wayne Thiebaud is a dream artist for dessert lovers. He represents those of us who still lick the frosting-coated spatula, believe that raspberries, chocolate, and lemon go with almost everything, and think of cakes, cookies, or ice cream as the perfect way to end a wonderful meal.

In the world of food, we are experiencing a very un-Thiebaudish trend. The glistening pastel cakes that are his signature would never contain the flavorings being used in desserts today, such as avocado, basil, and lemongrass. Even Thiebaud's clean-lined vision of how desserts are supposed to look—round and delicately decorated, by someone who was probably smiling—is being challenged by the popular belief that anything found at the end of the menu should resemble complex modern architecture, laboriously constructed by a team of grimacing pastry chefs. Wayne Thiebaud's art offers a tip to these culinary explorers. In the all-American imagination, desserts occupy sainted territory, and at the bottom of every urban appetite is the need for something quiet, sweet, and beautiful.

A DESSERT MENU

Animal Cookies

Ice Cream Sundaes with
Three Toppings

Devil's Food Cake with
White Mountain Frosting

Henri Matisse, *The Horse, the Equestrienne, and the Clown* (published 1947)

ANIMAL COOKIES

Makes 25 to 30 cookies

BEVERAGE SUGGESTION
Coffee and milk

2 *cups (4 sticks) unsalted butter at room
   temperature*
1 *cup granulated sugar*

1 *egg yolk*
3 ¹/₂ *cups unbleached all-purpose flour*

❈ Preheat the oven to 325 degrees F. Using a heavy-duty electric mixer fitted with the paddle attachment, beat the butter on medium speed until it whitens and holds stiff peaks, approximately 3 to 5 minutes. Beat in the sugar until combined. Turn the speed to low and add the egg yolk. Add the flour and continue to mix until a soft dough forms. Form the dough into a large ball, wrap in plastic wrap, and refrigerate for at least 1 hour or for as long as overnight.

❈ Remove the dough from the refrigerator and remove the plastic wrap. On a lightly floured work surface, roll out the dough ¹/₄-inch thick. Cut into animal shapes. Place the cookies 1 inch apart on an ungreased baking sheet and bake on the middle rack of the oven for 5 to 10 minutes, or until golden brown. Transfer to wire racks to cool. Repeat until the desired number of cookies is baked. Store any unused dough in plastic wrap in the refrigerator for several weeks, or freeze in an airtight container.

ICE CREAM SUNDAES WITH THREE TOPPINGS

Serves 6 to 8

VANILLA BEAN ICE CREAM
3 *cups heavy (whipping) cream*
1 *cup milk*
5 *vanilla beans*
8 *egg yolks*
$^1/_2$ *cup granulated sugar*

Hot Fudge Sauce (recipe follows)
Marshmallow Sauce (recipe follows)
Butterscotch Sauce (recipe follows)
Chocolate ice cream (optional)
Coffee ice cream (optional)
Whipped cream, for garnish
Toasted almonds, for garnish

If you do not have time to make the ice cream, a good store-bought version will do. I like to make this sundae with a scoop each of espresso, chocolate, and vanilla ice cream. But it is delicious with only vanilla ice cream. I like to serve it in a wineglass so that the contrasting colors of the sauces are visible.

❈ To make the vanilla bean ice cream, place the cream and milk in a large saucepan. Split the vanilla beans in half lengthwise, scrape their seeds into the pan, and then add the pods. Place over medium-high heat and scald the mixture. Remove from the heat, cover, and let the flavors infuse for 30 minutes. Meanwhile, in a large bowl, beat together the egg yolks and sugar for a few minutes until the sugar has dissolved and the mixture is thick and pale yellow; set aside. Reheat the cream mixture to scalding. Pour approximately one fourth of the hot cream mixture into the egg yolks, whisking continuously. Then whisk the egg mixture into the cream mixture in the saucepan. Cook over low heat, stirring constantly with a wooden spoon, until the mixture thickens and coats the back of the spoon. Remove from the heat and strain through a fine-meshed sieve into a bowl. Whisk a few times to release the heat. Allow to cool completely. When thoroughly cooled, freeze the custard in an ice cream maker according to the manufacturer's instructions. *Makes 1 $^1/_2$ quarts.*

❈ To assemble each sundae, place a scoop of chocolate (or vanilla) ice cream in a wineglass and top with some of the hot fudge sauce. Place a scoop of coffee (or a second scoop of vanilla) ice cream on top of the fudge sauce and spoon the marshmallow sauce over it. Next, place a scoop of vanilla ice cream on top and spoon the butterscotch sauce over it. Finally, crown with whipped cream and toasted almonds and serve.

HOT FUDGE SAUCE

Makes approximately 2 1/4 cups

7 1/2 *ounces bittersweet chocolate, cut into*
    2-inch pieces
1/4 *cup granulated sugar*
1/2 *cup light corn syrup*

1/2 *cup plus 2 tablespoons water*
3/4 *cups unsweetened cocoa powder*
2 *teaspoons instant coffee powder*
3 *tablespoons Cognac or brandy*

✳ Melt the chocolate in a heatproof bowl placed over a saucepan of barely simmering water. (The water should not touch the bottom of the bowl, or the chocolate will burn.) Turn off the heat and let sit over warm water until ready to use.

✳ Combine the sugar, corn syrup, water, cocoa powder, and coffee in a large saucepan and bring to a boil. Boil for 1 to 2 minutes, stirring constantly to keep the mixture from burning on the bottom. When the surface is covered with bubbles (and when you can no longer taste the graininess of the cocoa powder on your tongue), remove from the heat and whisk in the melted chocolate. Return the saucepan to the heat and boil for a few minutes until reduced to a mixture that is as thick and sticky as you like. The fudge will have a glossy shine. Stir in the Cognac or brandy and let cool slightly before using. This sauce will keep for several weeks in an airtight container in the refrigerator. To reheat, place the sauce in a bowl over simmering water.

MARSHMALLOW SAUCE

Makes approximately 2 cups

1 *cup granulated sugar*
1 *cup light corn syrup*
1/2 *cup water*

2 *egg whites*
1 *tablespoon vanilla extract*

✳ Combine the sugar, corn syrup, and water in a large saucepan and bring to a boil. When the mixture boils, it will throw sugar onto the sides of the pan. At this point, wash down the sides of the pan with a wet pastry brush, dipping the brush in water as necessary. Boil gently for 10 to 15 minutes, or until the mixture reaches the soft-crack stage (270 degrees F on a candy thermometer or when a small amount dropped into cold water separates into firm though pliable strands). Remove from the heat and set aside.

✳ Meanwhile, in an electric mixer set on medium speed, beat the egg whites until they are frothy. Then, while beating the egg whites, gradually pour in the sugar syrup in a steady stream until all of it is incorporated. Continue to beat the mixture until it is cool. The mixture should appear very white and fluffy. Gently fold in the vanilla extract using as few strokes as possible. Let cool at room temperature before serving. This sauce can be stored in an airtight container in the refrigerator for several weeks. Return to room temperature before serving.

Pablo Picasso, *Le Gourmet* (1901)

BUTTERSCOTCH SAUCE

Makes approximately 2 cups

1 *cup granulated sugar*
2 *1/2 tablespoons light corn syrup*
2 *1/2 tablespoons Scotch whisky*

1 *1/4 cups heavy (whipping) cream*
1 *vanilla bean*
1 *1/2 cups (3 sticks) unsalted butter, cut into pieces*

❈ Combine the sugar, corn syrup, and Scotch in a large saucepan over medium-high heat and cook, swirling the pan occasionally, until the mixture just begins to smoke and turns an amber color.

❈ Meanwhile, place the cream in another large saucepan. Split the vanilla bean in half lengthwise, scrape its seeds into the pan, and then add the pods. Add 1 cup (2 sticks) of the butter and bring to a boil. Remove from the heat and set aside until needed.

❈ When the sugar mixture reaches the proper color, immediately stop its cooking by whisking in the cream mixture in small amounts, waiting a few seconds after each addition to prevent boiling over. Once all the cream mixture is incorporated, simmer the sauce for 5 minutes. Whisk in the remaining 1/2 cup (1 stick) butter until combined. The sauce will keep for several weeks in an airtight container in the refrigerator. To reheat, place the sauce in a bowl over simmering water.

DEVIL'S FOOD CAKE
WITH WHITE MOUNTAIN FROSTING

Makes one 8-inch triple-layer cake; serves 8

2 tablespoons unsalted butter, melted, plus $^1/_2$ cup
   (1 stick) unsalted butter at room temperature

2 tablespoons plus $^1/_4$ cup unsweetened
   cocoa powder

2 $^1/_2$ ounces bittersweet chocolate, cut into
   2-inch pieces

4 tablespoons water

$^3/_4$ cup packed dark brown sugar

4 eggs, separated

$^1/_4$ cup sour cream

1 $^1/_4$ teaspoons baking soda

1 teaspoon boiling water

1 $^1/_4$ cups unbleached all-purpose flour, sifted

2 tablespoons granulated sugar

White Mountain Frosting (recipe follows)

❋ Brush an 8-inch round cake pan with some of the melted butter. Line the bottom of the pan with an 8-inch round of parchment paper or waxed paper. Brush the paper with the remaining melted butter and place the pan in the freezer briefly to solidify the butter. Dust with the 2 tablespoons of cocoa powder and knock out the excess. Set aside.

❋ Preheat the oven to 350 degrees F. Melt the chocolate in a heatproof bowl placed over a saucepan of barely simmering water. (The water should not touch the bottom of the bowl, or the chocolate will burn.) Turn off heat and let sit over warm water until ready to use.

❋ Whisk together the water and the remaining $^1/_4$ cup cocoa powder in a small saucepan. Bring to a simmer over medium heat, whisking constantly, until the mixture is smooth and thickened and the whisk leaves an empty trail when it is drawn across the bottom of the pan. Remove from the heat. Whisk in the melted chocolate and set aside in a warm place.

❋ Using a heavy-duty electric mixer with the paddle attachment, beat the $^1/_2$ cup butter on medium speed until it lightens and holds soft peaks, approximately 3 to 5 minutes. Beat in the brown sugar until well blended. Turn the speed to low and add the egg yolks, one at a time, beating well after each addition and scraping down the sides of the bowl as necessary. Beat in the chocolate and sour cream until well blended. In a small bowl or cup, dissolve the baking soda in the boiling water, making sure that the baking soda fizzes. Beat half of the flour into the batter, add the dissolved baking soda, and then beat in the remaining flour until well blended. Set aside.

❋ Using the electric mixer with the whisk attachment, beat the egg whites on low speed until frothy. Increase the speed to medium and beat until soft peaks form. Increase the speed to high and gradually beat in the granulated sugar until stiff, glossy peaks form.

❋ Whisk one-third of the egg whites into the chocolate mixture to lighten the texture, then fold in the rest, incorporating them well. Pour the batter into the prepared cake pan. Bake in the oven for 25 minutes, or until the cake shrinks slightly from the sides of the pan while remaining slightly soft in the center. Let cool completely on a wire rack.

❋ When thoroughly cool, invert the cake onto a rack and peel off the paper. With a serrated knife, trim the rounded top of the cake so that it is flat, and then cut cake horizontally into 3 even layers, each no more than $1/2$ inch thick. Place 1 cake layer on a serving platter or cardboard round, trimmed side up, and spread the top with a $1/8$-inch-thick layer of frosting. Place the second layer on top, press down lightly, and spread with the same amount of frosting. Top with the third cake layer and press down lightly. Spread additional frosting on the sides of the cake. Refrigerate for 30 minutes to firm.

❋ Place the cake on a cake stand or hold the cake flat on your palm for easy handling. Scrape the remaining frosting onto the top of the cake and spread it with a back and forth motion, using a long-bladed flexible metal spatula held flat against the top of the cake. Allow the frosting to flow over the edges of the top. When the top is smooth, use the spatula to spread the frosting down the sides of the cake in broad, smooth strokes, turning the cake after each stroke.

WHITE MOUNTAIN FROSTING

Makes approximately 2 cups, enough to frost a 3-layer 8- or 9-inch cake

2 cups granulated sugar
$3/4$ cup water
3 tablespoons light corn syrup

4 egg whites
2 teaspoons vanilla extract
$1/2$ teaspoon almond extract

❋ Combine the sugar, water, and corn syrup in a medium saucepan and stir over low heat until the sugar is dissolved. Bring to a boil. When the syrup boils it will throw sugar onto the sides of the pan. At that point, wash down the sides of the pan with a wet pastry brush, dipping the brush in water as necessary. Boil the mixture gently for 5 minutes, or until the syrup reaches the soft-crack stage (270 degrees F on a candy thermometer or when a small amount dropped into cold water separates into firm though pliable strands). Remove from the heat and set aside.

❋ Using an electric mixer set on low speed, whip the egg whites until soft peaks form. Then, while beating the egg whites, pour in the sugar syrup in a slow, steady stream until all of it is incorporated. Continue to beat the mixture for 2 to 3 minutes, or until the frosting forms firm rounded peaks that hold their shape. Gently fold in the vanilla and almond extracts using as few strokes as possible. Use the frosting immediately.

WORKS OF ART

Balthasar van der Ast
Basket of Flowers, c. 1622
Oil on panel
Gift of Mrs. Paul Mellon, *81*

Giovanni Bellini and Titian
The Feast of the Gods, 1514/1529
Oil on canvas
Widener Collection, *118*

Charles V. Bond
Still Life: Fruit, Bird, and Dwarf Pear Tree, 1856
Oil on canvas
Gift of Edgar William and Bernice Chrysler
Garbisch, *54*

Pierre Bonnard
Bouquet of Flowers, c. 1926
Oil on canvas
Ailsa Mellon Bruce Collection, *20*
© 1995 Artists Rights Society (ARS), NY/
ADAGP/SPADEM, Paris

Pierre Bonnard
Stairs in the Artist's Garden, 1942/1944
Oil on canvas
Ailsa Mellon Bruce Collection, *15*
© 1995 Artists Rights Society (ARS), NY/
ADAGP/SPADEM, Paris

Pierre Bonnard
Table Set in a Garden, c. 1908
Oil on paper mounted on canvas
Ailsa Mellon Bruce Collection, *2–3, 44–45*
© 1995 Artists Rights Society (ARS), NY/
ADAGP/SPADEM, Paris

Georges Braque
Peonies, 1926
Oil on wood
Chester Dale Collection, *31*
© 1995 Artists Rights Society (ARS), NY/
ADAGP, Paris

Georges Braque
Still Life: Le Jour, 1929
Oil on canvas
Chester Dale Collection, *9*
© 1995 Artists Rights Society (ARS), NY/
ADAGP, Paris

Mary Cassatt
Afternoon Tea Party, 1890/1891
Color drypoint and aquatint on laid paper
Rosenwald Collection, *56*
© 1995 Artists Rights Society (ARS), NY/
ADAGP, Paris

George Catlin
Green Corn Dance—Minatarrees, detail, 1861
Oil on paperboard
Paul Mellon Collection, *39*

Paul Cézanne
Still Life, c. 1900
Oil on canvas
Gift of the W. Averell Harriman Foundation
in memory of Marie N. Harriman, *35*

Paul Cézanne
Still Life with Peppermint Bottle, c. 1894
Oil on canvas
Chester Dale Collection, *69*

Marc Chagall
The Hen with the Golden Eggs, 1927/1930
Etching
Rosenwald Collection, *40*
© 1995 Artists Rights Society (ARS), NY/
ADAGP, Paris

Jean Siméon Chardin
The Kitchen Maid, 1738
Oil on canvas
Samuel H. Kress Collection, *112*

Jean Siméon Chardin
Still Life with Game, c. 1760/1765
Oil on canvas
Samuel H. Kress Collection, *74–75*

John Constable
Wivenhoe Park, Essex, 1816
Oil on canvas
Widener Collection, *27*

Joseph Decker
Grapes, c. 1890/1895
Oil on canvas
Collection of Mr. and Mrs. Paul Mellon, *114*

Joseph Decker
Green Plums, c. 1885
Oil on canvas
Collection of Mr. and Mrs. Paul Mellon, *8*

Raoul Dufy
The Basket, 1926
Oil on canvas
Chester Dale Collection, *16*
© 1995 Artists Rights Society (ARS), NY/
SPADEM, Paris

Henri Fantin-Latour
Still Life, 1866
Oil on canvas
Chester Dale Collection, *58, 59*

Paul Gauguin
Breton Girls Dancing, Pont-Aven, 1888
Oil on canvas
Collection of Mr. and Mrs. Paul Mellon, *88*

Paul Gauguin
Haystacks in Brittany, 1890
Oil on canvas
Gift of the Averell Harriman Foundation
in memory of Marie N. Harriman, *88–89*

Paul Gauguin
Self-Portrait, 1889
Oil on wood
Chester Dale Collection, *71*

Vincent van Gogh
Farmhouse in Provence, 1888
Oil on canvas
Ailsa Mellon Bruce Collection, *98*

Vincent van Gogh
The Olive Orchard, 1889
Oil on canvas
Chester Dale Collection, *96–97*

Childe Hassam
Oyster Sloop, Cos Cob, 1902
Oil on canvas
Ailsa Mellon Bruce Collection, *53*

Gerrit Willemsz. Heda
Still Life with Ham, detail, 1650
Oil on panel
Gift of John S. Thacher, *60*

Edward Hicks
The Cornell Farm, 1848
Oil on canvas
Gift of Edgar William and Bernice Chrysler
Garbisch, *109*

Winslow Homer
Fresh Eggs, 1874
Watercolor, gouache, and graphite on wove paper
Collection of Mr. and Mrs. Paul Mellon, *25*

Walt Kuhn
Pumpkins, 1941
Oil on canvas
Gift of the Avalon Foundation, *32–33*

Edouard Manet
Oysters, 1862
Oil on canvas
Gift of the Adele R. Levy Fund, Inc., *50*

Edouard Manet
The Plum, c. 1877
Oil on canvas
Collection of Mr. and Mrs. Paul Mellon, *46*

Edouard Manet
Still Life with Melon and Peaches, c. 1866
Oil on canvas
Gift of Eugene and Agnes E. Meyer, *107*

Edouard Manet
Two Apples, c. 1880
Watercolor over graphite
Collection of Mr. and Mrs. Paul Mellon, *92*

Master of the Catholic Kings
The Marriage at Cana, c. 1495/1497
Oil on canvas
Samuel H. Kress Collection, *122*

Henri Matisse
The Horse, the Equestrienne, and the Clown,
published 1947
Color stencil in gouache
Gift of Mr. and Mrs. Andrew S. Keck, *128*
© 1995 Succession H. Matisse, Paris/
Artists Rights Society (ARS), NY

Henri Matisse
Palm Leaf, Tangier, 1912
Oil and graphite on canvas
Chester Dale Fund, *66*
© 1995 Succession H. Matisse, Paris/
Artists Rights Society (ARS), NY

Henri Matisse
Still Life with Apples on a Pink Tablecloth, 1924
Oil on canvas
Chester Dale Collection, cover, *104–105*
© 1995 Succession H. Matisse, Paris/
Artists Rights Society (ARS), NY

Henri Matisse
Still Life with Pineapple, 1924
Oil on canvas
Gift of the Averell Harriman Foundation
in memory of Marie N. Harriman, *73*
© 1995 Succession H. Matisse, Paris/
Artists Rights Society (ARS), NY

Henri Matisse
Still Life with Sleeping Woman, detail, 1940
Oil on canvas
Collection of Mr. and Mrs. Paul Mellon, *134–135*
© 1995 Succession H. Matisse, Paris/
Artists Rights Society (ARS), NY

Claude Monet
Interior, after Dinner, 1868/1869
Oil on canvas
Collection of Mr. and Mrs. Paul Mellon, *144*
© 1995 Artists Rights Society (ARS), NY/
SPADEM, Paris

Claude Monet
Jerusalem Artichoke Flowers, 1880
Oil on canvas
Chester Dale Collection, *77*
© 1995 Artists Rights Society (ARS), NY/
SPADEM, Paris

Claude Monet
Woman Seated under the Willows, 1880
Oil on canvas
Chester Dale Collection, *19*
© 1995 Artists Rights Society (ARS), NY/
SPADEM, Paris

Berthe Morisot
In the Dining Room, 1886
Oil on canvas
Chester Dale Collection, *11*

Netherlandish
Head of Cabbage with Insects,
early seventeenth century
Watercolor
Rosenwald Collection, *117*

Pensionante del Saraceni
Still Life with Fruit and Carafe, c. 1610/1620
Oil on canvas
Samuel H. Kress Collection, *124*

Pablo Picasso
Le Gourmet, 1901
Oil on canvas
Chester Dale Collection, *1, 131*
© 1995 Artists Rights Society (ARS), NY/
SPADEM, Paris

Camille Pissarro
The Artist's Garden at Eragny, 1898
Oil on canvas
Ailsa Mellon Bruce Collection, *22–23*

Camille Pissarro
Orchard in Bloom, Louveciennes, 1872
Oil on canvas
Ailsa Mellon Bruce Collection, *28, 29*

Auguste Renoir
Girl with a Basket of Fish, c. 1889
Oil on canvas
Gift of William Robertson Coe, *100*

Auguste Renoir
Girl with a Basket of Oranges, c. 1889
Oil on canvas
Gift of William Robertson Coe, *100*

Auguste Renoir
Picking Flowers, detail, 1875
Oil on canvas
Ailsa Mellon Bruce Collection, *48–49*

Auguste Renoir
The Vintagers, 1879
Oil on canvas
Gift of Margaret Seligman Lewisohn in memory
of her husband, Sam A. Lewisohn, *110–111*

Jan Steen
The Dancing Couple, 1663
Oil on canvas
Widener Collection, *78*

Wayne Thiebaud
Cakes, 1963
Oil on canvas
Gift in Honor of the 50th Anniversary of the
National Gallery of Art from the Collectors
Committee, the 50th Anniversary Gift Committee,
and The Circle, with Additional Support from the
Abrams Family in Memory of Harry N. Abrams,
126, back cover

Henri de Toulouse-Lautrec
A Corner of the Moulin de la Galette, 1892
Oil on cardboard
Chester Dale Collection, *82*

Henri de Toulouse-Lautrec
Country Outing (Partie de campagne), 1897
Color lithograph
Rosenwald Collection, *12*

Antonio Maria Vassallo
The Larder, probably c. 1650/1660
Oil on canvas
Samuel H. Kress Collection, *121*

Maurice de Vlaminck
Still Life with Lemons, detail, 1913/1914
Oil on canvas
Chester Dale Collection, *103*
© 1995 Artists Rights Society (ARS), NY/
ADAGP, Paris

Antoine Vollon
Mound of Butter, 1875/1885
Oil on canvas
Chester Dale Fund, *85*

Edouard Vuillard
Repast in a Garden, 1898
Gouache on cardboard
Chester Dale Collection, *90, 91*
© 1995 Artists Rights Society (ARS), NY/
SPADEM, Paris

Edouard Vuillard
Two Women Drinking Coffee, c. 1893
Oil on cardboard on wood
Ailsa Mellon Bruce Collection, *43*
© 1995 Artists Rights Society (ARS), NY/
SPADEM, Paris

Edouard Vuillard
Woman in a Striped Dress, 1895
Oil on canvas
Collection of Mr. and Mrs. Paul Mellon, *62, 63*
© 1995 Artists Rights Society (ARS), NY/
SPADEM, Paris

Wagguno
Fruit and Baltimore Oriole, 1858
Oil on canvas
Gift of Edgar William and Bernice Chrysler
Garbisch, *64*

NOTES ON CONTRIBUTORS

RICK BAYLESS is an authority on Mexican regional foods. Raised in Oklahoma by a family of restaurateurs, he completed degrees in Spanish language and Latin American culture. As the host of the public television series "Cooking Mexican," he and his wife, Deann, traveled throughout Mexico, learning regional specialties made by local restaurants, market vendors, and street-stall cooks. In 1987 they opened the Frontera Grill in Chicago and in 1989, Topolobampo. He is the author of *Authentic Mexican* and *The Essential Mexican Kitchen*.

JULIA CHILD studied at the Cordon Bleu after World War II and taught cooking in Paris with Simone Beck and Louisette Bertholle. The first volume of *Mastering the Art of French Cooking*, which introduced the American public to the techniques of French cooking, was published (with Beck and Bertholle) in 1961. Her television series, "The French Chef," was launched in 1963. Among her many books are *Julia Child and Company, From Julia Child's Kitchen, The Way to Cook*, and *Cooking with Master Chefs*. Born in Pasadena, California, she graduated from Smith College. Prior to her marriage to Paul Child, she worked for the OSS in China and Ceylon.

PATRICK CLARK began his culinary training at New York City Technical College and apprenticed with Michel Guerard at Les Pres et Les Sources d'Eugenie, Les Bains, France. He opened his own restaurant, Metro, before becoming executive chef at the Hay-Adams Hotel, Washington, D.C., and he is now the executive chef at Tavern on the Green in New York. He has long been active in efforts to help establish culinary scholarships for African Americans.

MARION CUNNINGHAM, a champion of simple American food, is the editor of the revised *Fannie Farmer Cookbook* and the author of *The Breakfast Book* and *The Supper Book*. Her writing about food has been widely published, and she contributes a column to the *San Francisco Chronicle* and the *Los Angeles Times*. She lives in Walnut Creek, California.

SUSAN FENIGER and MARY SUE MILLIKEN, both classically trained, are co-chefs and proprietors of the Border Grill in Santa Monica, California. They are the authors of *City Cuisine* and *Mesa Mexicana*, which present their eclectic blend of traditional and ethnic influences, and hosts of the public radio show, "Good Food."

DEBORAH MADISON founded the landmark vegetarian restaurant, Greens, in San Francisco. She is the author of several books on vegetarian cuisine, including *The Greens Cook Book, The Savory Way*, and *Vegetarian Joy*. Her articles have appeared in *Saveur, Cooks Illustrated*, and *Food and Wine*, and she is a guest instructor at cooking schools throughout the country. She lives in New Mexico.

LORENZA DE' MEDICI is the author of over 30 cookbooks, including *The Heritage of Italian Cooking, The Renaissance of Italian Cooking*, and *Tuscany* and *Italy the Beautiful* cookbooks. She has appeared in a 13-part series on Italian cooking for public television, and she conducts a cooking school at Badia a Coltibuono, the eleventh-century abbey and wine estate of her husband, Piero Stucchi-Prinetti, in the Chianti region of Tuscany, near Siena. Born and raised in Milan, she traces her ancestry to Lorenzo de' Medici.

JOËL ROBUCHON and PATRICIA WELLS are co-authors of *Simply French*. Robuchon, a pioneer of *cuisine moderne*, opened Jamin in Paris, which became a Michelin three-star restaurant in two years. He is now the chef and owner of Restaurant Joël Robuchon in Paris. Wells, an American, is the only foreigner to have been restaurant critic for *L'Express*. She is the author of *The Food Lover's Guide to Paris, The Food Lover's Guide to France, Patricia Wells' Trattoria*, and *Bistro Cooking*. She lives in Paris and Provence with her husband, Walter Wells, who is news editor of the *International Herald Tribune*.

NANCY SILVERTON began her formal training at the Cordon Bleu in London and attended the Ecole Lenotre in Plaisir-Grignon, France. She and her husband, Mark Peel, are co-chefs and owners of the restaurant Campanile and the La Brea Bakery in Los Angeles. She is the author of *Desserts* and *Mark Peel & Nancy Silverton at Home*.

JEREMIAH TOWER earned a master's degree in architecture at the Harvard Graduate School of Design before becoming a chef. He took a "temporary" job as chef at Chez Panisse in the 1970s and stayed for six years. There he was instrumental in shaping the "California cuisine" revolution. *Jeremiah Tower's New American Classics* was published in 1986. He has several restaurants including Stars and Stars Cafe in San Francisco, Stars Oakville Cafe in the Napa Valley, and Stars in Palo Alto.

ALICE WATERS founded the legendary Chez Panisse in Berkeley, California. Known for revolutionizing American cooking with the innovative use of local, seasonal ingredients, she is the author of numerous cookbooks, including *The Chez Panisse Menu Cookbook, Fanny at Chez Panisse, Chez Panisse Cooking* (with Paul Bertolli), and *Chez Panisse Pasta, Pizza, and Calzone*. Born in Chatham, New Jersey, she studied French culture at the University of California, Berkeley, and was a Montessori teacher before opening the restaurant in 1971.

PAULA WOLFERT is a leading authority on Mediterranean cuisine. Her first cookbook was *Couscous and Other Good Food from Morocco*. It was followed by *Mediterranean Cooking, The Cooking of South-West France, Paula Wolfert's World of Food*, and most recently, *Cooking of the Eastern Mediterranean*. She also contributes frequently to *Food and Wine*, the *New York Times*, and *Gourmet*.

METRIC EQUIVALENTS

Liquid Weights

U.S. Measurements	Metric Equivalents
$1/4$ teaspoon	1.23 ml
$1/2$ teaspoon	2.5 ml
$3/4$ teaspoon	3.7 ml
1 teaspoon	5 ml
1 dessertspoon	10 ml
1 tablespoon (3 teaspoons)	15 ml
2 tablespoons (1 ounce)	30 ml
$1/4$ cup	60 ml
$1/3$ cup	80 ml
$1/2$ cup	120 ml
$2/3$ cup	160 ml
$3/4$ cup	180 ml
1 cup (8 ounces)	240 ml
2 cups (1 pint)	480 ml
3 cups	720 ml
4 cups (1 quart)	1 litre
4 quarts (1 gallon)	3 $3/4$ litres

Dry Weights

U.S. Measurements	Metric Equivalents
$1/4$ ounce	7 grams
$1/3$ ounce	10 grams
$1/2$ ounce	14 grams
1 ounce	28 grams
1 $1/2$ ounces	42 grams
1 $3/4$ ounces	50 grams
2 ounces	57 grams
3 ounces	85 grams
3 $1/2$ ounces	100 grams
4 ounces ($1/4$ pound)	114 grams
6 ounces	170 grams
8 ounces ($1/2$ pound)	227 grams
9 ounces	250 grams
16 ounces (1 pound)	464 grams

Temperatures

Fahrenheit	Celsius (Centigrade)
32°F (water freezes)	0°C
200°F	95°C
212°F (water boils)	100°C
250°F	120°C
275°F	135°C
300°F (slow oven)	150°C
325°F	160°C
350°F (moderate oven)	175°C
375°F	190°C
400°F (hot oven)	205°C
425°F	220°C
450°F (very hot oven)	230°C
475°F	245°C
500°F (extremely hot oven)	260°C

Length

U.S. Measurements	Metric Equivalents
$1/8$ inch	3 mm
$1/4$ inch	6 mm
$3/8$ inch	1 cm
$1/2$ inch	1.2 cm
$3/4$ inch	2 cm
1 inch	2.5 cm
1 $1/4$ inches	3.1 cm
1 $1/2$ inches	3.7 cm
2 inches	5 cm
3 inches	7.5 cm
4 inches	10 cm
5 inches	12.5 cm

Approximate Equivalents

1 kilogram is slightly more than 2 pounds
1 litre is slightly more than 1 quart
1 meter is slightly over 3 feet
1 centimeter is approximately $3/8$ inch

INDEX

INDEX

Claude Monet, *Interior, after Dinner,* detail (1868/1869)